INNER
STRENGTH
INNER
PEACE

Life-Changing Lessons
From the World's Greatest

Tim McClellan

Budo Inc.

Library of Congress Cataloging - in - Publications Data.
McClellan, Tim
Inner Strength Inner Peace: Life-Changing Lessons From the World's Greatest

Budo Incorporated
2815 E. Libra Street
Gilbert, AZ 85234

Cover photo acknowledgements:
Gary Hall Jr. (Photo by Tim Clary/AFP/Getty Images)
Pat Tillman (Photo by Gene Lower/NFL/Getty Images)
Stacy Dragila (Photo by Alexandr Satinsky/AFP/Getty Images)
Donovan McNabb (Photo by Stephen Jaffe/AFP/Getty Images)
Jessi Colter (Photo by Charles Gaurean)

www.StrengthAndPeace.com

DEDICATION

Special thanks to all of my friends and acquaintances who have served to strengthen my inner peace and my resolve.

Most of all, thank you to my wife, Janet. My dear friend, Kevin "T-Bone" Dee, often tells me, "You would be nothing without Janet." T-Bone, I agree.

ACKNOWLEDGMENTS

SAMANTHA WEISS - EDITOR

I have often said I may not be smart, but I know smart. Samantha is a genius and has been an invaluable asset to me by doing the bulk of the editing. Samantha graduated from MIT with a B.S. in chemical engineering, and another in writing. She is currently in graduate school studying computational fluid dynamics. Her aspirations are to earn a Ph.D. and to author several books. Thank you, Samantha, for your patience and tolerance. Samantha can be reached at Samantha.F.Weiss@gmail.com.

YAWNA ALLEN - COPY EDITOR

I have had the privilege of training Yawna as she starts her professional tennis career. Yawna graduated with a B.A. in news-editorial journalism from Oklahoma State University, where she starred on the Cowgirls tennis team. Yawna can be reached at YonahDaye@aol.com.

SARAH "IRON CHILD" HEDBERG - PHOTO EDITOR

It has been a blessing for me to have had the opportunity to train Iron Child over the past three years. I have also been fortunate to have her expertise in editing all of my photos, including some very old ones. Iron Child was a 2009 Arizona State High School Champion in the pole vault, and is now enjoying college track. She has been like a daughter to me.

KRISTLE SCHULZ - TYPE SETTER

Kristle is another athlete I have had the privilege of training, and another example that I know smart. Kristle is a stand-out student and volleyball player at Xavier College Preparatory in Phoenix, Arizona. Her computer skills, patience and work ethic were a tremendous asset to this project.

JULIA VANHELDER - COVER DESIGNER

I have seen Julia grow from an eight-year-old with crooked bangs in the judo dojo, to a professional young woman. Her hard work and creativity in designing the covers shows her immense talent. Julia can be reached at judosuperstar@gmail.com.

COURTNEY EKMARK - WEB DESIGN

Over the course of thirty years of coaching I have not found a more focused athlete than Courtney. Simply put she will work longer than others and harder than others and will be a star both on and off the basketball court. Her drive and ability to achieve the desired outcome made her the logical choice for my Web site design.

CONTENTS

INTRODUCTION

There is an often recited quote used in many martial arts programs to foster the personal development of the students. It says, "Imagine that every person in the world is your teacher, and think how smart you would be if you learned from them. Surely everyone you meet has something they could teach you."

Along these lines, I feel like I have been blessed. I have had many teachers from all over the world. Many were very high-achieving athletes who dominated the sporting world for years. Others were very philosophical martial artists and instructors, some of the finest in the world. Some, like my self, were in a position to coach athletes to greater success. A few were young people that I helped to guide and mentor. Yet others were noted celebrities, psychologists, accountants, salesmen, marketers, and even a few canines.

The purpose of this book is not to recount funny stories or quirky people. It is not to self-glorify through association with the rich or famous. Rather, the purpose of this book is to illustrate the blessing that my teachers have been in my life. It is my hope that these stories will help you recognize and receive those in yours.

Tim McClellan

Chapter 1

ANSWERING YOUR INNER CALLING
PAT TILLMAN

"There was never a question where Pat Tillman stood. The character of a man is a very valuable thing...the character of a man is his ability to make a decision and stand by it. Pat defined the word character."
-Dave McGinnis, Former Arizona Cardinals Head Coach

Pat warming-up before one of his pre-boot camp workouts, aside Julie Fisher (Chapter 8). This is known as "the lull before the storm".

Courageous. Loyal. Intelligent. Brave. Caring. Heroic. Friendly. Humble. Committed. Patriotic. Every youth should aspire to this list of virtues. Some will take a lifetime just to achieve a few of them. Some will never perfect any. Pat Tillman achieved all of them. These are not my words to describe Pat; these are all quotes from others. Pat's story has been well documented.

Five years after his death in 2004, Pat Tillman's face could still be found on the front page of newspapers nationwide. His story, for those who haven't heard it, is this: Pat played professional football for the Arizona Cardinals.

He'd established a Cardinals all-time single season record for number of tackles and had been offered a three-year $3.6 million contract to remain with the team. He turned it down. Instead of playing for the NFL, he was moved to pursue a career as an Army Ranger, for a salary of $18,000 and the opportunity to crawl around in the dirt and get shot at in Afghanistan. I cannot imagine anyone else making that choice. In doing so, he lost his life.

Entire books have been written about Pat Tillman, most of them by sports writers and columnists who did not know him well. I knew him well. I was Pat's strength and conditioning coach during his first year at Arizona State University. Years later, he came to me and his former triathlon coach, Jim Rosania, and—after swearing us both to secrecy—told us he'd decided to leave the NFL to follow an inner calling, the one that led him to Afghanistan. At the time, he'd told only his immediate family and the two of us. He asked us to train him for war; he wanted to be in better shape than anyone else entering the Army Ranger School. During the eight weeks that followed, with the exception of a brief honeymoon trip—he'd just gotten married to an exceptional woman, Marie—I trained Pat six days a week.

Columnists often wrote that Pat seemed too small to be a decent college linebacker. Yet he earned the honor of PAC-10 Defensive Player of the Year. Similarly, he seemed an unlikely professional player, despite his talent. These articles usually cite that Pat turned down a five-year, $9 million offer from the St. Louis Rams, because loyalty compelled him to stay with the Arizona Cardinals. As he saw it, the Arizona Cardinals had drafted him and had been the first team to believe in him. As most others saw it, the Arizona Cardinals had offered him far less money and would almost certainly be a losing football team year after year. Yet Pat succeeded in becoming a well-known professional player. A few articles note that while others in the NFL spent exorbitant amounts of money on lavish cars, Pat usually rode his bicycle to practice. That was Pat as I remember him—humble—and utterly determined to uphold his values and achieve his goals.

All of these stories about Pat are true. But they are not the ones foremost in my heart. The ones foremost in my heart, the ones I feel best exemplify Pat's character, are the ones I actually had the blessing of living through.

The first story takes place three years into Pat's career in the NFL. It was fall, and football season. I hadn't seen Pat for six years. I was attending one of Roland Sarria's "Rage in the Cage" shows, a mixed martial arts event. I know lots of athletes, and martial artists in particular, and so I often bump into people I know at these things. This night was no exception. I was conversing with a small crowd of people I hadn't seen for months, and in the periphery of my vision was Pat, in a plain white t-shirt and a pair of blue jeans. This was the same Pat Tillman who had played an unbelievable game the week before, making big headlines. He stood behind the group and looked in my direction as though waiting to talk. I remember thinking to myself, "This guy's an NFL star. I'm sure he's not waiting to talk to me." Once I had convinced myself of that, I continued my conversation. After fifteen full minutes, he quietly stepped forward, stuck out his hand to me and said, "Coach McClellan, I'm Pat Tillman and I played for you, do you remember me?" I was floored. Of course I remembered Pat. He had worked his butt off for me when I coached him. I always described him as the type of guy you'd want beside you if you were stuck in a foxhole in a war. Besides, if I hadn't remembered him, all I would have had to do is pick up the paper any day that previous week; his name had made headlines almost every day for his standout play the week before. This was Pat: humble, thoughtful, loyal, and an NFL hero, all rolled into one.

The next time I spoke to Pat was a year or two later, when he came to Jim "J.R." Rosania and I, to ask for help preparing for boot camp. J.R. and I had collaborated on a training program for Pat. This included five days of high intensity circuits, including standard military items such as push-ups, squat thrusts and sit-ups. It also included our own protocols, which were varying intensities of fartlek intervals. In more common terms, we put the future Ranger candidate through hell on the treadmill, running up hills at speeds and gradients that would put his body in a physiological state near blacking out. This can happen when blood glucose levels in the brain drop significantly. Pat wouldn't have it any other way. He asked J.R. and I to give him a great amount of work because he wanted to be his best. That was the only way he knew. Pat's desire would out-perform his body.

As part of his training I brought Pat to Chuck Coburn's Shotokan karate dojo on Saturdays and Sundays. I tried my best to not only condition Pat through grappling, kicking, punching and throwing, but also to teach him the hand-to-hand combat maneuvers he would need to know. One particularly hard-driving Saturday morning, Pat landed in the choke hold of Mark Brown, a Phoenix police officer, who was also the former captain of the Arizona State University football team and had been my judo training partner for years. The next thing I knew, Mark was yelling Pat's name over and over again, and louder each time. He had choked Pat unconscious, and was trying to wake him up. That was Pat, pushing everything to its limit. He knew Mark had the chokehold effectively applied, and he had plenty of time to tap out and get Mark to release the hold. But Pat was Pat and he was going to push things as far as he could.

Later that day, toward the end of the workout, he and I fought several ju-jitsu matches and he wasn't able to pull off the throws he wanted to. He approached my wife Janet, and I watched her demonstrate some techniques for him. At the time, Janet was in her early 40's, 5'4" tall, 125 pounds and only a brown belt. The room was filled with both talented black belts and other big, strong, fast, skilled beasts like Mark Brown, who had not yet achieved the black belt rank. After the workout, Janet told me Pat had asked her for help with his koshi guruma. Koshi guruma is a Japanese name for a judo throw where—simply stated—one person head locks another and throws the other person over their hip. Pat had tried this on me several times, and found that instead of being

6

the guy doing the throw, he would end up being the guy thrown.

"Why would Pat go to Janet?" I wondered. He could have asked me. He could have asked any of the other male black belt participants. But to Pat, the guy without the ego, it didn't matter where the information came from. He simply wanted to be at his best. The information didn't have to come from the highest ranking black belt. He knew Janet could provide him with the guidance he needed. In asking her, he afforded her with the highest of compliments: his trust. In doing so, he taught me several lessons about being free of ego, being humble, and striving to bring out my very best.

People often wonder why Pat would give up millions of dollars and an NFL career to fight as an enlisted man and to take orders from nineteen-year-old kids in the process. That's easy for me to explain. Pat had an inner calling. Pat knew football is a game and freedom is a privilege. Pat knew that the country, both its people and values, were more important than the number of interceptions he had at the end of the year. As his former head coach Dave McGinnis said, "Pat knew his purpose in life. He proudly walked away from a career in football to a greater calling, which was to protect and defend our country." If only more people would answer their inner calling and pursue them the way Pat did, regardless of the nature of that calling, this world would be a much better place. Pat's value system, conviction, and courage are things I wish I could teach all of the young athletes I coach. I believe that Pat is a guardian angel. I can no longer tell him how much I appreciate the life lessons he taught, but if I could, I would write him the following letter (knowing Pat and his sense of humor, he'd bust out laughing):

> Dear Pat,
>
> I hope you are doing well now that you are with Jesus. I imagine you are, since you both had the same hairstyle and the same strength of conviction. I miss our times in the dojo, but you're not far from my heart. I've embroidered the number forty

onto the top of my karate uniform. It's illegal to do so, but I'm bending the rules just a little bit, kind of like you always did. It's not to draw attention to you. I know you wouldn't like that. Rather, it's to keep you, your convictions, your courage and your friendship close to my heart. It's to remind me of what we all should be. You fought for us, so I fight for you.

I have little doubt in my mind that Pat Tillman knew exactly what he was getting himself into when he left the NFL and joined the Army Rangers. Before he left for boot camp, I asked him to sign an autograph, the first time in twenty years I had ever asked an athlete I coached to sign for me. I am not sure why I did so. I am just honored to have it today. When Pat signed that, he concluded with, "take care of yourself." To me, the finality of his writing suggested an awareness of what his fate might be. What he probably did not know was how special he was as our role model. He was my friend and my teacher, and his spirit still serves me as a guiding light. May your ways be with us forever. May others follow their inner calling with the strength and conviction that you did.

As Jake Plummer, his ex-teammate and star quarterback said, "To honor Pat, we should all challenge ourselves." Amen.

(Photo by Gene Lower/NFL/Getty Images)

Chapter 2

THE BLESSING OF DISCOMFORT
SENSEI ANDY BAUMAN

"I guess it's gonna have to hurt, I guess I'm gonna have to cry, and let go of some things I love to get to the other side."
-From the Carrie Underwood song, "Starts With Goodbye"

Sensei Bauman (4th from left) and his crew of animals. Since it was my birthday, he awarded me (3rd from left) with a special present: the 20 pound weight vest. The tiger on the wall says it all about Andy Bauman and Ja Shin Do intensity.

For many people, pleasure drives most waking moments. Life is a quest to fulfill the desire for pleasure. At times, the consequences of pleasure seeking can be so immense that it can change a person's life forever. The desire for pleasure often overrides rational thought.

Mentally walk through a day in your life if you'd like to know just how often the desire for pleasure consumes you. For instance, you wake up in the morning on a comfortable mattress, perhaps even one of those Sleep Number mattresses that allow you to precisely dial the perfect amount of pleasure. Your pillow is comfortable. The blankets you selected provide you with exactly the right amount of warmth, as does the thermostat you set to precisely the degree that will keep you happiest. The newspaper is delivered, so you don't have to go anywhere to get it. Most breakfasts are either instant, or picked up without ever having to leave the car. To further ensure pleasure, your taste buds have chosen the morning meal. Even though the billions of other cells in the body may not crave that sugar-coated, fat-laden cinnamon bun, the pleasure seeking taste buds, the minority, have made the call. The morning shower is taken with the most pleasing water temperature. Shaving is done with the "smooth and comfortable" razor. The softest cottons and linens are worn. Then it's into the car, which is probably more expensive than you could have paid for similar transportation, but is much more comfortable. You dial in the exact temperature and the most pleasing music. And this goes on hundreds of times throughout the average day.

While pleasure seems to be a never ending pursuit, it should not be the only pursuit, according to martial arts master Andy Bauman. Andy runs an eclectic martial art called Ja Shin Do, which means, "path of self-belief." It may be the hardest training a person can go through. Trainees of Ja Shin Do submit themselves to a physical and mental training regimen second to none, and the experience can only can be described as bittersweet. The intensity of the challenge invokes hatred, and yet the sense of accomplishment is intoxicating.

I was coaching at Arizona State University when I first heard about Ja Shin Do. Jeff Funicello, one of our collegiate wrestlers, suggested I go to Ja Shin Do class for the ultimate workout. He gave me Andy's number. Being a hard-training martial artist already, I was looking forward to trying a new dojo and seeing a different style. "Be early," Jeff said. "This is real serious stuff. Andy Bauman was born from discipline, and he'll demand the same of you." So, one hot summer morning I made arrangements to meet Andy. I had heard similar—usually exaggerated—stories about other dojos I had visited. I was young, strong, fit, and training like a machine, so I didn't have exceptionally high expectations.

I threw about seven hundred side kicks that morning, and all with the right leg. I threw the same number of side kicks with my left leg. That is, we threw one side kick, then two, then three, etc. until we hit twenty-five. And then we went back down to one, those were only the side kicks. We also threw front kicks and round house kicks. We did a thousand and ten repetitions of abdominal exercises. The workout lasted about two hours. By the time I finished, I'd also done over two hundred push-ups and a large number of the martial arts training techniques, often while holding bricks in my hand.

I lost the skin on all eight of my fist knuckles and experienced a mental challenge that would leave an impression for life. Ja Shin Do was truly different. The class was to start at 9:00 a.m., but 9:00 a.m. Ja Shin Do time was 8:50. Fifty of anything by Ja Shin Do count was actually fifty-one. Ja Shin Do prides itself on always doing more. Everything we did was more: more kicks, more punches, more blocks, more conditioning, more mental challenge. Rest was the only thing that was not "more." In fact, rest was totally absent. Apparently, rest must have showed up at 8:52 a.m., and was locked out of the dojo, like everyone body else that was there after 8:50.

People would ask me, "Why on Earth would anyone want to go through that?" My first thought is that the challenge is immensely gratifying and unexplainable. My second thought is of a John Wooden analogy. John Wooden is known by many as the most successful coach ever to live. His UCLA basketball teams won the NCAA title ten times in his tenure as head coach. John Wooden told his players never to mistake activity for achievement. This is a simple, but profound, idea. I have been to dozens of dojos with plenty of activity, but not much mental growth or self-conquest. I have watched athletes train frequently, but without the intensity necessary to improve performance.

I usually find that my words are inadequate to convey the Ja Shin Do workouts or Andy Bauman's intensity. And so I end up quoting what he said to me after class that day while I put Bactine on my knuckles:

"Tim, do you feel a sense of accomplishment? If I had asked you before class if you wanted to throw fourteen hundred side kicks, do over a thousand reps of abdominal exercises and do hundreds of push-ups in addition to the martial arts work, would you have said yes? I'm sure you wouldn't have, but I can tell by looking at you, that you are glad you did. This is the essence of true martial arts, and of life, and the ancients knew this. A warrior's constant companion is inner strength. Never forget this. There are thousands of martial artists that have pretty kicks, but few have developed their inner strength to its potential.

This is the important part. It is this inner strength that should govern your daily life, the strength to be strong when you feel weak, the strength to be courteous when others would not be, the strength to help others when it is not necessarily your responsibility. It is this inner strength that should be with you at all times, both in and out of the dojo.

So how does one develop this inner strength, Tim? It has to be through challenging times. Plato said the greatest conquest of all lies within one's self. This is something very few can achieve, but if you can achieve this, helping others is easy. The very pain we all run from is essential in learning this. Everyone wants to get away from pain, challenging times and things that society deems un-pleasurable. Think back about your life, and the lives of others you have known. I'll bet you'll find that most any time they had an un-pleasurable experience, that significant growth occurred as a result of it. The tough times help people to grow, to strengthen their resolve. Without them, society would merely get soft, and there's no growth in lying around in comfort twenty-four hours a day. Without challenge and mental growth there can be no true happiness. It comes down to realizing that pain, in most cases, is a blessing because it brings growth. People need to learn to embrace the things that help them grow, not run from them. The excess of kicks today was such pain, but if I ask you now if you would have rather had a workout where you threw only ten kicks, you'd say no. This type of training is indispensable in one's accomplishment of growth."

Indeed I gained new perspective on facing discomfort. Since then, I've made myself do something I don't like every day. Little things, like drinking green tea, taking cold showers, and stretching. In that way I teach myself not to avoid discomfort, a mentality that has empowered me tremendously. It could have only happened through the strenuousness of an Andy Bauman workout.

Thank you Andy for being my friend, and more importantly, for caring to be my teacher. My life is better because of the pain I experienced in your classes. I have learned the blessing of discomfort and will cherish the lesson the rest of my life.

Chapter 3

OUTWORKING OTHERS

KURT ANGLE

"Do not in any circumstance, depend upon a partial feeling."
-Miyamoto Musashi

1996 Olympic Champion Kurt Angle at the awards ceremony in Atlanta.

In my pursuit to become an effective strength and conditioning coach, the greatest blessing has been the diversity of experiences I have had along the way. To date, I have been fortunate enough to coach the highest paid quarterback in pro-football, the fastest swimmer in history, a World Champion boxer, an All-Star short stop, the top mixed martial art fighter on the planet, the highest fielding second baseman in baseball, the top sumo wrestler in the world, a track athlete that set dozens of World Records, and the WWE Champion professional wrestler. That wrestler was none other than Kurt Angle.

Kurt Angle wasn't always the WWE World Champion. Once upon a time, back in the early 1990s, he wasn't on the radar as an aspiring amateur wrestler. At that time, Kurt's weight class, the 220 pound limit, was stacked with beasts.

Mark Coleman won the 1992 World Team Trials, and represented the United States in the 1992 Olympic Games. Mark Kerr, a phenomenal athlete, unseated Coleman in the weight class to become the United States representative in the 1994 World Championships. Dan Chaid, among others, gave Coleman and Kerr all they could handle in their annual battles. All in all, it was a stacked class. Kurt Angle, the chubby kid from Clarion, Pennsylvania, didn't make the top of anybody's list.

That was about to change, and for one reason: Kurt Angle outworked the rest of the world. This isn't to say Coleman, Kerr, Chaid, and the rest of the beasts didn't do their fair share of work, they did. And like them, Kurt worked hard and diligently, but he apparently found the over-achiever formula for success.

I met Kurt at the 1996 Olympic training camp, and he asked me to help him with strength and conditioning. I interviewed Kurt, took down his history, and together we planned a strategy for optimizing his performance. He made it clear he would do whatever I felt necessary to win the Olympic gold medal.

This seemed like a bit of a gamble on his behalf. Before the meeting, he didn't know me at all. He had never worked under my guidance or followed any of my exercise prescriptions. He had already become the top wrestler in his class in the World Championships in 1995, and seemed to have found his formula for success. I had the impression he was so focused on winning he never thought to doubt or distrust me. I found it a strangely heavy responsibility to meet a guy and have his lifelong dream placed in my hands within minutes. I decided that if Kurt Angle had no doubt in me, I wouldn't either. I would do everything in my power to help Kurt in his pursuit of Olympic gold.

The wrestlers selected to represent the United States were grown men, and some of them had been champions or medalists in World Championships. I was there to guide those in need, but not to run a mandatory high-school type program. Most opted to work with me, and some simply avoided extra strength and conditioning training. Others, like Kurt Angle, came to me every day after practice, regardless of how injured, tired or beat up. Kurt was receptive and followed whatever I thought would bring out his best. Kurt trained with me every day, even after exhaustive practices. Kurt went heavier in some weights, at my request, than he had ever gone before. Kurt went lighter in weights, at times, then he normally would, at my request. Regardless of the work I requested, Kurt Angle delivered.

He went into the Olympic Games well prepared. The sport is so competitive at this level that any one of a dozen competitors could easily have won the gold medal. I certainly thought Kurt had a chance, but with former World Champions in the class, I thought such a win would be tough.

Kurt Angle won the Olympic gold that week, in a historic match over Abbas Jadidi of Iran. It was one of the hardest fought victories in the history of the sport. And some of the takedown defenses twisted Kurt's body in positions that seemed impossible. The photographs that appeared in *USA Today* the next day were astonishing.

Kurt Angle did not win the Olympic gold medal because of my strength and conditioning programs. I didn't wave the magic wand over him. Kurt Angle won his Olympic gold medal because he outworked the rest of the world, both that day and every day, transforming himself from the chubby kid from Clarion. I like to think Kurt Angle benefited from his time with me, but I'll always know how much I benefited from the lesson he taught me. If the chubby kid from Clarion can outwork the world and make dreams come true on the biggest stage of them all, then others can do the same.

Chapter 4

PERSONAL ACCOUNTABILITY

"FLIP"

"Discipline yourself, so others don't have to."
    -John Wooden

1976 photo of Coach Tom Filipovits holding junior slot receiver Tim McClellan (#87) accountable for his assignments on the field. This was not the only time. (Photo by 1977 Parkland High School Yearbook Staff)

In this age, society's sensitivity seems to be increasing rapidly. Little League Baseball has been replaced by "T-ball," so every kid can hit the ball and none suffer the mental anguish of a strike out. Many children no longer receive letter grades in school, so average "C" students can feel higher self-esteem, instead of feeling merely "average." Kids constantly seek validation from their parents and siblings, and parents seem to go out of their way to validate their kids, even when the efforts and outcomes don't seem to merit the rewards and excessive praise.

I did not grow up in that era. I grew up in a much different era. In my era, a student who did average work received C's as grades. Students who excelled earned A's, and poor performance earned lower grades.

Tom Filipovits was my high school football coach. Like many other coaches, the quality of his work exceeded his compensation. In fact, he coached so well that the words he used during our grueling practices in the autumn of 1977 are still alive in my mind, three decades later. "You are responsible for your outcome on the field, and in life," he said to us, again and again. "Demand a great deal of yourself. Accept responsibility for your actions."

I remember these words not only because "Flip" preached them so many times, but because he led by example. He ran every step we ran and lifted every set and repetition we lifted, often with twice as much weight. He was unyielding in his demands on us, and unyielding in his demands on himself.

In 1977, our high school, Parkland High, played a close game against Allentown Central Catholic. At the time, we had a new player starting at the center position on offense, Mike Koch. As is common with those without extensive experience, his play was inconsistent. As we drove down the field toward the goal line, trying to score the touchdown that would put us in charge of the game, John Miksits, the head coach, called a play that required us to run the ball outside of the right tackle. Mike had a simple assignment: to snap the ball and shield the backside linebacker from running all the way across the field to make the tackle. This was a pretty easy block to make.

Mike's path was unobstructed, and the guy he had to block was no superstar; it doesn't get much better than that. We were sure to get the first down and take command of the game. That never happened. Our running back was tackled for a two-yard loss and the drive was stalled. I remember making a great block and looking up from the ground in amazement to find we had lost yards on the play. I wondered how that could have happened. It wasn't until the next day, when we reported to get our "grades," that I knew.

Flip gave us a grade on each play, a real grade, not a feel-good-about-yourself grade. If you got a four, you put your opponent flat on his back. If you saw a three, it was a very good block. You got a two for an average job,

19

a one for a poor job, and zero if you were a zero. Flip held us all accountable. Everyone on the team could read what you did on every play and there was no faking. We didn't always like the grade, but it helped us improve.

I'll never forget looking at my score on that play. I had earned a four. I knew I had driven my man from his feet, directly onto his back. Sometimes things just go your way. Then I wanted to know why the play broke down. Who was the weak link? Greg Kloiber had a three. So did Glen Skawski. "How could this go wrong?" I wondered. Then I saw it. Next to Mike Koch, the scribble in red said, "-1," with the never-before-seen comment, "unbelievable, unforgettable, unforgivable."

From that day on, Mike asked me to stay after practice every day for a few minutes to practice the skill he had failed. He accepted accountability for his failure, something Flip had taught us. With focused work during and after practices, he had an amazing senior season, one that far exceeded expectations. Had Flip not taught us that WE are directly responsible for OUR outcomes, neither one of us would have been successful.

In the same way, Flip was responsible for my transformation from a 148 pound, third-string wide receiver as a junior, to a strong, fit, 200 pound offensive lineman as a senior. Had anyone told me, as a junior, that I would make all-conference honors, the all-star game, and be recruited to play college football, I would have never believed them. Only Flip could have made that happen. Indeed, he taught me that, "Discipline isn't something you do to someone; it's something you do for someone." Thank you, Flip, on behalf of the thousands of kids you've coached. You have taught us well to hold ourselves accountable to appropriate standards. You've transformed my life forever. You taught me well. I love you.

30 years later and I still feel the sense of accountability.

Chapter 5

CONSIDERATION
DONOVAN MCNABB

"What lies behind us and what lies in front of us are small compared to what lies within us."
    -Anonymous

(Photo by Stephen Jaffe/AFP/Getty Images)

A few years back, I decided to switch from car radio to informative CDs during my commutes to and from work. At some point, I heard Stephan Covey's CD, "The Eighth Habit", in which he differentiates between primary greatness, a person's integrity, character, morals, and values, and his secondary greatness, his accomplishments, honors, awards, and recognitions. Covey encourages people to strive for primary greatness. Only after I listened to "The Eighth Habit" was I able to describe Donovan McNabb.

I have had the privilege of training quarterback Donovan McNabb for eight off-seasons. Every sports fan knows Donovan McNabb has plenty of secondary greatness. Donovan was an accomplished quarterback at Syracuse college, and part of the Syracuse team who went to the Final Four in basketball. He was one of the top picks in the NFL draft. He led his team to the Super Bowl. He played in several Pro-Bowls. He signed the contract that made him the highest paid quarterback in the game. The list goes on.

I have been fortunate enough to see the other side of Donovan, the primary greatness. In the summer, my business associate, Warren Anderson of Rehab Plus and I often encourage college and a few high school players to jump in and train with the two dozen or so NFL players. Donovan welcomes them all into the group, shakes their hands, asks them to tell him something about themselves, and assigns them hilarious nicknames. We've had "Ben Affleck," "Joe Millionaire," "Shaggy," "The Thing," and "Hamburger," amongst others. He shares stories about his life and tips for getting better, and treats each kid like the most important person on the planet. Any high school quarterback, no matter their skill level, always seemed to benefit from Donovan's coaching. I find it amusing that not everyone recognizes him, and yet he seems to know and love everyone.

One Tuesday morning, we did some indoor hill training on the treadmills. Donovan will be the first to tell you that hill training day will never be confused with a good day. The more the merrier is our philosophy on hill training day. There is nothing like elevating a treadmill to fifteen degrees, setting the speed to fifteen, and seeing how long a player can grind through burning legs and lungs. Donovan has done more of his fair share of hill training.

About three-quarters of the way through the Tuesday session, Donovan had to go a little longer than usual to stay ahead of the rest of the pros. He is ultra competitive and always tries to win such contests. When he finished, he got off the treadmill and immediately flopped to his back on the floor, dripping sweat that resembled a rain shower. I thought he would start to hyperventilate and I actually felt sorry for him. This workout bordered on inhumane. For those that wondered what a guy like Donovan McNabb does in the off-season, I can tell you it can be brutal. I can't speak for most other NFL quarterbacks, but the ten or so that I have trained in the off-seasons have all shown me how they've reached the highest level of their profession.

Lying on the floor and all but hyperventilating, Donovan caught sight of an elderly lady with a walker coming toward the door to enter for physical therapy.

One of many times Donovan has worked himself into this state for us.

Donovan sprung to his feet and opened the door for her. I felt a moment of guilt that this poor guy, who I had near death, had beaten me to it. I expected Donovan's obligation to end there, but I was wrong.

"Good morning ma'am," he said to the elderly woman. "Thank you for coming today. How has your morning been?" This continued on until he actually escorted her all the way down through the gym to the back corner to the rehab area. Others in his profession may have played in the Pro Bowl, and I've worked with dozens who have, but I didn't ever expect to see an act of consideration like that again. I was wrong.

The following Thursday, Warren and I were out on the field running the group, the group that should have included Donovan. He was visibly and audibly absent. An hour and a half later, when we returned to the weight room at Rehab Plus, Donovan came to open the door for us.

"Tim, one of your kids came in while I was icing my ankle. Since you weren't here, I trained him for the last hour and a half."

I have to admit, I thought it was a joke and so I gave him a "Thanks Donovan. I'm sure you did better than I would have." Only two days later did

9th grade baseball player Joey Bielek come and tell me that he was personally trained by Donovan for over an hour. I was floored.

That same summer, my then eighty-year-old mother visited from Pennsylvania. Since she lives near Philadelphia, she read about Donovan all the time, especially the articles and national media publications about me training him. She never would have had the opportunity to meet him in Philadelphia. During one particularly hot, hundred and five degree workout, I asked my wife Janet to bring my mother to see the running session. My mother had never seen me at work. Thirty minutes into the workout we gave time for a water break. I had never asked Donovan for a personal favor because he must get thousands of those requests per year. But this day during the break I asked him if he would meet my wife and mother.

"I already did," he said.

I should have known better. Donovan is considerate to everyone. Talk to our professional, collegiate, and high school players, and they will tell you they love Donovan McNabb. Talk to people who grew up in his hometown, like Simeon Rice, and they will tell you they love Donovan McNabb. Talk to Ann Frederick, his stretch therapist at Stretch to Win, and she'll tell you how much she loves Donovan McNabb. Everyone who knows Donovan appreciates his character and integrity. At a time when his secondary greatness starts to fade, his primary greatness will remain.

Thank you, Donovan, for being so much more as a person than you are as a quarterback. And by the way, you're an amazing quarterback.

Chapter 6

▲

PASSION

RACHEL, KELLY, AND THE HUSKIES

"Human beings are made so that whenever anything fires the soul, impossibilities vanish. A fire in the heart lifts everything in your life."
    -John C. Maxwell

Rachel Mittelstaedt became a client of mine when she entered Xavier College Preparatory in Phoenix, Arizona. I coached her throughout her successful high school volleyball career, culminating in two first team All-State awards, a regional Player of the Year award, a team State Championship, and a top fifty national recruits ranking. When she signed her scholarship papers to play in the PAC-10 Conference, I felt proud.

Kelly Burrell was also a client of mine. Like Rachel, Kelly was an all-state setter from Xavier College Prep. She was honored as top player in Arizona, and led her team to State Championship titles. When she signed her scholarship offer to play for the incomparable Debbie Brown at the University of Notre Dame, I couldn't have been happier. My wife and I loved these two girls like daughters.

Madison is an Alaskan husky who lives on a glacial field in Juneau, Alaska. It's a far cry from the scorching heat of Phoenix, and Madison's education was a bit different than the one Xavier Prep provided.

Normally, it's not acceptable to compare someone else's children to a dog, but with apologies to Reed and Beth Mittelstaedt and Roger and Carol Burrell (the parents, and my dear friends), I'm going to do just that.

May 26, 2004 was my twentieth wedding anniversary, and I wanted to plan a unique trip for my wife Janet. Because Janet has been the most amazing wife anyone could ever dream of having, I knew I wanted to do something special for her in celebration. If it were any other vacation, I would have booked a trip to the Club Med we found in San Salvador, Bahamas, but I wanted to honor Janet for all she is to me. Finally it came to me. I decided on the one thing she has always wanted to do and I have never had any desire to do: take an Alaskan cruise.

The dog lover that she is, I knew Janet would enjoy taking a dog sled ride, so we booked one in Juneau for our anniversary date. To get to the dogs, we flew by helicopter over miles of majestic glaciers. Upon arriving, we were awed by the beauty of the countryside and the dogs. We asked of we could pet the sled dogs, and to my surprise, the sled operator said, "No." Then she explained, "These dogs were not bred to be house pets. Like their ancestors, these dogs were bred to run sleds. They really don't want to be petted, they want to run the sled."

They pulled a sled up to the line of dogs that would run us. While the other dog lines (more than a hundred dogs) lay sleeping or at least acting docile, our line went ballistic. They knew by the sled's placement that they were about to run. They were ecstatic. This one in particular, a little girl named Madison, seemed even more excited than the rest. She was frantically barking, wagging her tail, and running in circles. There was nothing she would rather do than be hooked up to that sled for the grueling run. Seeing any being, canine or otherwise, seem that passionate is quite the sight for a coach whose primary goal is to enhance people's passions.

Madison (on left): ready to run

Until that day, I always sought to understand how Rachel and Kelly seemed to have such extraordinary passion as compared to others. They were so easy for me to coach. I barked orders; they did as asked, to the best of their ability, one hundred percent of the time. It wasn't always easy for them, especially when I took them to run in hundred and ten degree weather. They endured bouts of puking, and at times, the work gave them both migraines. Kelly's headache once hit her so hard she fell asleep on

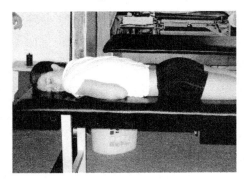 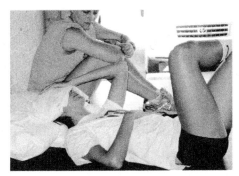

the treatment table after a workout. Rachel had a migraine so bad we had to ice her head for twenty minutes before she could even see properly. She had done jump squats that day until she literally had tears running down her face. When I asked her why she didn't just stop, she said, "Because you told me to do twenty more." They did reps and reps and reps, sometimes in fireman turn-outs. If

Rachel was one hot trainee--literally!

they could do it while sweating that profusely, volleyball games would be easy for them.

Why would these two girls go through the crazy training that most linebackers wouldn't go through? Why would they continue to do this for so many years? Both had so much going for them, and surely could have earned academic scholarships. Really, they wouldn't even need academic scholarships; both families were wealthy. Typical teenage girls do not repeatedly workout until they puke, squat 'til they drop, and run until they cannot breathe.

Madison answered my questions about Rachel and Kelly. It was passion. Passion drove them to achieve things they were not destined for. Neither Kelly or Rachel had the genetic traits conducive to elite athletics, but both excelled as elite athletes. They worked longer, worked harder, never once told me they could not do what I asked of them. I coached hard and they worked hard, and they accomplished big things. I often wondered why these two girls were so different than the thousands of others I have coached, athletes who were merely extremely hard workers. Without speaking a word, Madison answered my questions.

Passion transforms the ordinary into the extraordinary. I have been blessed to observe the example of Rachel and Kelly time and time again, over many years. Through their example I try to bring that same passion to my martial arts training, and it gives me a competitive edge.

Thank you Rachel; thank you Kelly. For the rest of your lives, the two of you can look back and know you probably pushed your athletic endeavors as far as your physiological potential would permit. Thank you for sharing the passion.

Chapter 7

TOLERANCE

GARY HALL JR.

"Great spirits have always encountered violent opposition from mediocre minds."

-Albert Einstein

I remember hearing stories about Gary Hall Jr. Stories, upon stories, upon stories. I heard these stories long before I met Gary. Without knowing him, I always tried to let the stories go in one ear and out the other. I just didn't feel it fair to judge a man I had not met. However I admit I was intrigued by how much this guy was talked about.

"Gary Hall Jr. is aloof." "Gary Hall Jr. doesn't work hard." "Gary Hall Jr. is not a coachable athlete." "Gary Hall Jr. is cocky." These are the

(Photo by Tim Clary/AFP/Getty Images)

things I was told about Gary Hall Jr. before I had met him. I was left with the impression that this guy was a nut.

While this story is not about me, I have to preface that I am indeed a nut magnet. Some guys get to be chick magnets. I am a nut magnet. I attract nuts. I used to say that if a nut came to town, I'd attract him, but my range has increased exponentially. I can now attract nuts from all over the world, and at this rate, I am sure nuts from outer space are not far behind. Once I heard how much of a nut Gary was, I had this feeling that we would meet.

The day came that Gary entered my life. His first swim coach, Pierre LaFontaine, recommended that Gary talk to me about strength training and conditioning. Pierre asked if I would be interested in training Gary and said he would arrange the meeting. We met later that day. Quite frankly, I came away from the meeting a little surprised. This young man who I thought would be one more nut in my life turned out to be just the opposite.

Gary Hall Jr. is not aloof. He is not cocky. Over the course of the eight years I coached him, he worked exceptionally hard. If you're one of the sports fans clinging to past sensationalized comments about Gary Hall Jr., forget them. I hate to disappoint you, but I am going to set the record straight.

Gary Hall Jr. is a humble young man who would rather talk about the fish he caught than the ten Olympic medals he earned. Talk to him about spear fishing or cleaning up the use of performance enhancing drugs in sports and you will have a long, lively, heart-felt conversation with a charming young man. Try talking to him about his Olympic gold medals and you'll have a brief conversation with a humble man who will barely maintain eye contact with you. In fact, the two times I have tried to speak with Gary about the five gold medals he won ended the exact same way: with him trying to give me one, telling me that I should really have one for the work I have done to help him. That's not the thought process of a cocky man. That's the thought process of an amazing man.

Furthermore, Gary Hall Jr. has worked his butt off for me. At times I've worked him so hard that his glucose levels dropped dangerously low and he had to leave the workout to get them back to an acceptable standard. This usually happened during a three-a-day workout, which includes two hard training sessions with his swim coach, Mike Bottom, and one with me. Every

time Gary Hall Jr. worked to this point, he came back hours later and asked me if he could finish his workout. This is not the sign of a lazy man. This is a sign of an overachiever. It's hard enough to win one Olympic medal, let alone five gold and ten total, while fighting diabetes at the same time. But Gary has found a way to do so. He doesn't have a mild

The one and only Gary Hall Jr. with coach Mike Bottom.

form of diabetes either. He has severe diabetes. Further, to know Gary is to love Gary. And I can honestly say he one of the kindest, gentlest, most appreciative, funny, and caring human beings I have ever met. From offering me his gold medals to sending me care packages full of Olympic memorabilia after each of his conquests, he has been nothing but one the best friends and trainees a man can have. I am blessed to have been able to work with such an incredible talent, but even that pales in comparison to the blessing of having a person like that in my life.

So, what lesson did Gary Hall Jr. teach me? He taught me the lesson of tolerance, for I envy his ability to put up with all of the public misrepresentations about who he really is. And why are there misrepresentations? Gary is a realist. He has been swimming his entire life. He is a boxing fan, a mixed martial arts fan, and a football fan. He has seen how these sports are marketed and the public appeal they have earned. He has seen fights in which boxers made $25 million dollars per bout. He has seen Super Bowl broadcasts go out to hundreds of countries. He has also participated in huge swimming events that were poorly attended and telecast via tape delay weeks after the event. Swimming just doesn't hold the appeal of the other sports in this country at this time. Gary is sharp, and he knows sports have changed throughout his lifetime and that extreme sports are gaining public appeal while old-fashioned sports are becoming neglected. To draw interest back to his passion - swimming - Gary will throw on a red, white, and blue boxing robe and shadow box before getting on the starting blocks at the Olympics. For his creativity, genius, and insight—for trying to keep swimming afloat in the public eye—he gets chastised for being different. Different. What a shame this amazing person has to get chastised for being different. After all, isn't it the different one who becomes  the Olympic gold medalist, who becomes the fastest swimmer on earth? Shouldn't he strive to be different? Why on earth does the media seem to start the witch hunts when it comes to Gary—is it because he's different?

Think back to the 2004 Olympic Games controversy, when Gary said the Americans in the 4x100 relay would smash the Australians like guitars. Wasn't he portrayed as an arrogant egotist? It's just too bad these reporters, looking for a sensational story, didn't do their jobs diligently. If they had, they would have found that Gary's comment was not pointed at the Australian swim team, but that it was a joke he had *with* the Australians, since he had just given Australian Michael Klem his own personal guitar that was worth over a thousand dollars, to congratulate him for swimming so well in a previous event. Yes, Gary gave a foreigner his cherished guitar to celebrate the other's great accomplishment. No one else in swimming, and probably no one else in sports, would have done so. Yet, he was hanged by the media. The reporters simply could have asked him the story behind the guitar quote. True to his class, Gary never mentioned a word. He just continued on his humble path, loving others and swimming really fast.

I feel bad for Gary that the whole world cannot know the man I know, but I guess if they did, I would not have learned the lesson of tolerance. Gary Hall Jr., you were the fastest swimmer in the fastest event. You swam faster in a legitimate race than anybody in the history of the world. That made you undoubtedly, at that time, the fastest swimmer ever. Only your character and tolerance exceeds your swimming ability. I am blessed to have you as my teacher and my friend.

Gary Hall: hardworking, fun, and tolerant.

Chapter 8

ANYONE CAN
JULIE FISHER

"Success is the peace of mind, which is a direct result of self-satisfaction in knowing you did your best to become the best that you are capable of becoming."
-John Wooden

At the end of her first workout, I didn't think an athlete-conditioning coach relationship would last between Julie Fisher and I, but I felt compelled to give it a second shot. I was no more confident after the second workout, or even the third. Had anyone come along and told me this girl would become a daughter-figure and my teacher I would have laughed.

Almost a decade ago I received a phone call from Lorie, Julie's mother. There is no mistaking that Lorie is the sweetest woman on the planet. Lorie seemed to be the kind of person to give you the shirt off her back, and in later years actually volunteered to do so, in addition to offering us her seat cushion, sun glasses, food, water, and her coffee. God just hasn't created a sweeter, more giving person.

When I first spoke to Lorie she was inquiring about hiring me to help Julie. At that time, Julie ran cross country and track as a freshman at Desert Vista High School. She had run a competitive 5:10 mile and belonged to a nationally ranked cross country program. As is common with young girls, she underwent a growth spurt and her times slowed, rendering her less competitive. Other runners on her team were seeking professionals to get a competitive edge, and Julie followed suit.

I liked her right away, and responded to her happiness and enthusiasm. She told me she would do whatever necessary to run better. We went out to the track, where I taught her a dynamic warm-up sequence and form-running drills. Then I asked her to run eight hundred meters for me. What I saw wasn't pretty. Although petite as a person, Julie was a little too big to be a stand-out distance runner. Worse, she lacked the natural explosion of energy that I like to see in an aspiring athlete. To top matters off, she was mechanically inefficient. She ran with her buttocks sticking back too far behind her hips, a sign of weakness, and she would flip out her right foot awkwardly. Too big, too slow, and mechanically inefficient—it was not a good combination.

From there we progressed inside to the treadmill. I would have to get her running fast up hills to help her. I also used the opportunity to find out how tough she was, and how committed she was when tired. I set out to make her tired. I elevated the treadmill to grade fifteen and set the speed to ten. Julie would have to run her butt off or do a face plant on the belt.

We were surrounded by giant NFL players, including Anthony Clement at 6'8" and 340 pounds, LJ Shelton at 6'6" and 350 pounds, and John Tait at 6'6" and 320 pounds. Just before she stepped on the belt, Julie got this nervous laugh and used body language that indicated discomfort. I told her I would not coach a timid, not-fully-committed athlete, and asked her if she wanted to continue. She said yes, so I ran her until she hyperventilated.

The second workout went about the same. She disappointed me again with nervousness and lack of focus, and I had the sense she wasn't the sort of athlete I wanted to coach. I knew I would have to work her into the ground to divert the misplaced attention. Again, I ran her until she hyperventilated. I made the workout much worse than the first. I thought I'd seen the last of Julie

Fisher.

"Are you coming back next week, Julie?" I asked, after ten minutes of trying to get her breathing back to normal.

"Absolutely," she said. "I want this really badly."

I was pretty sure she wouldn't want to come back. The severity of the workout would have made almost anybody quit, especially someone that sweet. I also knew that with her larger frame, poor mechanics, and no natural speed, I would have to train her like that for many years for her to have a fighting chance of getting to the level she dreamed of. I wondered how long she would last.

It wasn't until many years later that I had the answer to that question. She would last with me until her last collegiate race was over, until the intense, focused, competitive running was done. Julie graduated with a 3.9 grade point average from Northern Arizona University (NAU), where she made All Conference honors twice in track and twice in cross country. She was an integral part of the team that ranked as high as third nationally in the National Collegiate Athletic Association; it was against all odds

This isn't just a story about a sweet girl and a happy ending, though. This is a story about how Julie worked—really worked—to make all of that happen. I would have her run twelve, quarter-mile sprints in freezing weather and hail storms at night. I demanded birthday workouts at midnight and also at 4:30 a.m. at times, workouts which included fourteen miles of running, most of it hard intervals. This is a story about hyperventilation episodes, too many to list, and about a girl who boxed, broke boards, and gave up junk food.

She achieved rare self-discipline throughout countless hours of demanding mental and physical training, and she retained that self-discipline throughout the rest of her career. As a sophomore at Northern Arizona University, she ran in the Big Sky Conference Championships, which were held at the rival school, Weber State. The teams knew they would be neck-and-neck, and Weber felt this particular meet, being a home meet, was their best chance to knock off perennial powerhouse NAU. Julie ran the 5000 meters and was in 11th place with one lap to go. She knew she was that far back, but if she could place 8th she could score a point for her team. She wanted so desperately to score a point that she started her kick too early. She passed to move into 10th and saw two Weber State girls in front of her. She knew what she had to do. She had to sacrifice herself for the good of the team. She passed number 9. As she tried to catch number 8, she literally dove across the finish line, voluntarily hurling her limp body face down onto the track. She did pass number 8 at the finish. The medical personnel came to escort this bleeding, hyperventilating girl who had done something no one else in that meet would have done, deliberately throwing themselves into bodily injury to score one point for her team by finishing 8th.

Julie is a devout Catholic, and I never knew with her whether there was divine intervention or just good karma. But Northern Arizona University scored 189 points that day, and the two runners from Weber State that crossed the finish line much more comfortably were on a team that scored 188 points.

For many years, this is the way Julie's races ended--with her near lifeless on the track, having given her all.

This wasn't a freak event in Julie's life. Results like this happened all the time. They happened, not because of talent, but because Julie Fisher would simply make herself do more things right than others, regardless of how difficult the challenge. She inspired herself with Navy Seal training tapes. On the tapes,

the Seals were required to run into the freezing ocean then roll on the sand to increase personal discipline. They called this "getting wet and sandy". On her own accord, Julie did this on her family vacation, when the ocean was too cold for others to go in. She also studied the "mind over matter" martial arts documentaries of people walking on burning coals, lying in glass, and breaking cinder blocks. When her team ate a pre-game meal of only pasta, she would beg her parents to drive her to the far side of Flagstaff so she could buy a chicken sandwich, and—as per my instructions—have protein with her carbohydrates. Then she would pull out the grilled chicken and throw the unhealthy white bun away.

At the conclusion of the 21st birthday run in Las Vegas at 1:30 am.

It's true that Julie spent her 21st birthday in Las Vegas. I know because I was in Las Vegas as well. I was out on the track with her at midnight, fulfilling our seven year annual tradition of having her accomplish something special on that day.

Julie was not that one-in-a-million born-to-be-an-athlete. She simply knew what she wanted and was willing to do what it took to succeed. Today, having completed her doctorate in physical therapy, Julie applies the same principles to all that she does. In doing so, she has served me not only as a trainee, but also as a daughter-like figure, beloved friend, and role model. Indeed, anyone can, if they are willing to pay the price.

Julie Fisher: All-Conference runner, all heart.

Chapter 9

PREPARING TO WIN WARS

SENSEI RAY

"It must be emphasized that to win, one must learn not only the principles of the art, but also the formation of the mind."

-From the martial art documentary "Budo"

Ray Hughes, arguably the meanest fighter on earth, hitting yet one more of his students, Jason Berbaum.

Years back, I had a long conversation with a United States Army Lieutenant. He had done several tours of duty in combat and was finishing his twentieth year of active duty. He was ready to re-enlist for twenty more. On top of being in the Army, he had been a martial artist for two decades and immersed himself in the warrior philosophy and mentality. When I asked him the difference between the U.S. Army soldiers and warriors of futile Japan, he told me, "The difference between night and day." How could that be? In my mind, a warrior was a warrior.

"Tim," he said. "Any of those fighting in today's army trained for about a year before they went to war. The samurai warrior of twenty-four years of age had been groomed for twenty-four years to be a warrior. From birth on, every cell of that samurai's body was prepared to do battle. It was this way twenty-four hours a day. Those fighting for the U.S. Army are courageous wonderful people but they have not been prepared for war like the samurai were."

At that moment, I understood what Sensei Ray Hughes had done for me. He had taught me to prepare for war.

I first started training with Sensei Ray two decades ago. Even before I started training with Sensei Ray, I had heard many stories about him, from many sources. Somewhere in each of these stories each person had mentioned that Ray was the meanest fighter on earth. In fact, if my memory serves me, that comment seemed to apply not just to Sensei Ray as a martial artist, but to Sensei Ray in general. The bottom line: this guy was mean. My friend and training partner at another dojo, Jason Berbaum, had been beaten up by Sensei Ray for years, and he had a slightly different take on it. "He's way better than you are, so if you fight him, you're going to lose. If you fight hard you'll lose, but he'll respect you and he'll help you. If you don't fight hard, you'll lose, he won't respect you, and he won't want to help you. Therefore, you're better off just fighting him hard."

That first night I took a class from Sensei Ray we sparred together, and I threw some haymakers to show him I was fighting hard. At one point, I lost visual contact with him and then I saw his glove coming at my nose from the side, whizzing right by my eye. Then my head snapped violently to the left, and my nose spewed blood everywhere. My nose wasn't just broken, it was very broken. For a few moments it was also quite crooked, until Sensei Ray told me I must have busted my nose and he grabbed onto it and snapped it into place. In case you are wondering, it hurts more to have your nose punched out of place than snapped back in. At this time, my secret dislike of Sensei Ray began. At the same time, I felt compelled to train under his guidance. He had phenomenal skill and a warrior's mentality, and I knew he would help me and probably change my life. I wasn't happy with him at that moment, but I knew I would continue to train with him and that I would learn from him.

Sensei Ray taught me to kick and punch. He also insulted my abilities as no one else has. He peppered my face with punches, most often with his left hand. At times, everyone I knew heard how much I disliked this man. Ray Hughes demanded perfection of Tim McClellan. Ray Hughes accepted nothing less. He demanded punctuality, focus, my best effort on every punch and every kick. He told me when I wasn't perfect. He told me when I wasn't even good. He never sugarcoated the truth. I pushed myself beyond what I thought were my physical limits. I pushed myself beyond what I thought were my mental limits. I got knocked down, and learned to get up like a warrior. Most of all I was given a piece of Sensei's heart. Sensei Ray didn't just take us through class, he taught us things far beyond the mechanics of kicking and punching.

He taught us to " show no pain." "Never show your opponent your fatigue or pain." Then, there were Sensei's favorites: "Die going forward. Don't ever die in retreat," "There is no excuse for inadequacy," and "Even if you have great fighting skill you have to prepare your mind. You have to exhibit good etiquette. This is the way the Samurai, the greatest warriors in the history of mankind, trained. They were ruthless when they fought but always in the strictest of etiquette when they weren't in battle."

Sensei Ray was paid to give us instructions on how to kick and how to punch. Yet, because he cared so deeply, because he was so passionate, so fanatical about teaching right from wrong, about teaching philosophy of a more appropriate way of life, he gave us so much more than just biomechanical feedback on how to better punch or kick somebody. Every martial artist involved in a striking art has received technical instruction on how to better perform. I would be willing to bet, too few have ever been blessed to take away lessons they could apply to their daily lives to better themselves as citizens and as warriors. These are the things that were taught to the Samurai for decades before they went to battle.

These are the things that have been demanded of me for decades by a very mean fighter who came from Globe, Arizona. For taking the extra time, for demanding so much, for helping me exceed pre-conceived limitations, I have to say Sensei Ray you are indeed worthy of the honor of being called Sensei. It is through your lessons that I have helped to change the spirits of hundreds of male and female athletes outside of martial arts. You gave me not only a piece of your fist but also a piece of your heart and it is something I will share with others for the rest of my life.

And by the way my nose is still crooked. Sensei, you do a much better job as a trainer of warrior spirit than you do as someone who fixes noses.

It was never about winning when Sensei Ray put the gloves on to fight. It was about the complete and utter obliteration of the opponent.

Chapter 10

FIGHTING YOUR BATTLES
CHRISTOPHE LEININGER

"It is not the critic who counts, not the man who points out how the strong man stumbles or where the doer of deeds could have done them better. The credit belongs to the man who is actually in the arena, whose face is marred by dust and sweat and blood, who strives valiantly, who errs and comes short again and again because there is no effort without error and shortcomings, who knows the great devotion, who spends himself in a worthy cause, who at the best knows in the end the high achievement of triumph and who at worst, if he fails while daring greatly, knows his place shall never be with those timid and cold souls who know neither victory nor defeat."

-Theodore Roosevelt

Sensei Ray had put me through many years of physically and mentally draining workouts, as he was trying to cultivate a dauntless spirit. After years and years of this, I found myself always wanting to remain a part of Wado-Ryu karate, but also becoming more intrigued by other martial arts, such as judo.

The premise of karate is to strike opponents, or would-be attackers, with punches, various kicks, knees, elbows or other means. In my eyes, judo was a natural compliment, as its principles are to grab and throw an opponent, and to either choke him unconscious, place him in a restraining pin, or apply an arm lock against the natural anatomical function of a joint (which, if applied too vigorously, hyper-extends the joint causing ligament tear and dislocation.) I saw these two arts as complementing each other, so I set off to find myself judo instruction.

Tom and Tawni Palen taught at the first judo dojo I attended. Classes were informative and workouts somewhat easy. This appealed to me after years of super-charged fighting workouts with Sensei Ray. I thought I would develop judo skills without going through hell to accomplish it.

Around this time, my friend Doug Hyde sent me to Christophe Leininger's dojo. He said Christophe sold the best gis (judo uniforms) in town, and that his dojo ranked top in Arizona. Christophe's students always fared the best in judo tournaments, and had the most honed skills. I gave Christophe a call and arranged to buy a gi from him later that week.

The dojo overwhelmed me. Photos of Christophe lined the walls— Christophe at the World Championships, at the Olympic Trials, on the winner's platform of the National Championships. Medals he had won from the National Championships hung everywhere. Totaled, I think he retired with thirteen or more of them. That feat is all the more amazing because judo is not like boxing, powerlifting, or karate, in which there is a so-called National Championship or World Championship hosted by a variety of organizations. In judo, only one true National Championship exists, and Christophe either won or placed in the top three in that championship over a dozen times.

I chatted with Christophe and he impressed me with his humility. He told me he would help me become proficient if I would willingly do the work. I had instant respect and admiration for Christophe, and so I went to get dressed for the workout.

I think I lost nine pounds that night. I later learned that Christophe was not the only national-class competitor at the dojo. They all were. In fact, several were National Champions, and all won multiple Arizona State Championships and Regional Championships. To top it off, they all saw new guys as bodies to be thrown, choked, and arm-barred. I was strong (from competitive powerlifting, weightlifting, and my karate black belt training), and so I essentially had a bulls-eye on my forehead. They knew I was strong and athletic, and had no inclination to hold back on me, not at the Leininger dojo. Kindness and other niceties were just not permitted there.

One of hundreds of arm bars Christophe put me in. This was a nightly occurance in the Leininger dojo.

I got done with that first workout and sat in the locker room, near dehydration. I had not planned on this for my judo education. But I knew at that moment that I would never allow myself to train under anyone else. I had ten or more fierce, national-class black belts trash me that night, but I had also seen Christophe beat every one of them. I figured if he knew how to conquer these seemingly unconquerable beasts then I could learn from him. The fact that he got in there and fought the battles made the difference for me.

Over the next five years, many top mixed martial arts fighters—who are not part of Christophe's dojo—asked me for help with strength and conditioning. No shortage of talent have made this request: I was a pretty good candidate for this job, as I coached elite athletes for a living, had done ten years of obsessive compulsive striking and years of throwing and submission skills. Mark Kerr, Mark Coleman, Kevin Jackson, Kenny Monday, Mike VanArsdale and Townsend Saunders were some of the world class athletes seeking my guidance. These were the top freestyle wrestlers and they were becoming the top mixed-martial artists of their era. As part of their comprehensive training program, I took all of them up to the Leininger dojo, because Christophe had knowledge and technical skills they could learn from. Mike VanArsdale was 215 pounds of pure muscle. He was slick, polished, and moved like lighting.

He could conquer any sport, and in fact won the World Cup championship in freestyle wrestling, and the Ultimate Fighting Championships. Mark Coleman was a 245 pound ex-Olympic wrestler, who had just bench pressed nineteen reps at 315 pounds. He was the Ultimate Fighting Championships Heavyweight Champion. Mark Kerr was the 250 pound version of Coleman and VanArsdale. He was the Pride Fighting Champion, and considered the world's most dominant fighter. Kevin Jackson and Kenny Monday were Olympic gold medalists. Both won the Extreme Fighting Championships, at a time when the event attracted tougher fighters than the Ultimate Fighting Championships.

While there was alot of diversity there for a long period of time, one thing remained constant: Christophe Leininger fought them all. He never let one pass through his dojo without a fight, no matter how sick he was, how tired, or how many yards of tape he had to put on his toes, fingers, or ankles. He fought them all. I saw him take down Mark Kerr. Some nights he couldn't get out from under Mark Coleman. One night, VanArsdale was on fire and threw Christophe, the National Judo Champion, repeatedly. Yet, Christophe accepted every challenge, without fail, without excuse. He stepped in every night of the week to fight his own battles. He never uttered a word about his own competence, but his actions spoke volumes about how he had become a judo legend. He did not merely drill judo or learn judo. He fought every guy he could possibly fight, especially the best this world offers. I saw him throw Kerr, submit Coleman, and arm-lock VanArsdale.

A little adage says, "I'd rather see a sermon than hear one, any day." Christophe Leininger showed me a sermon every day, and his courage to step up and fight his own battles will serve to guide me for the rest of my life.

Earning rank under Christophe Leininger is one of the difficult and meaningful things a martial artist can do.

Chapter 11

▲

PURPOSE

JOHN BECK

"To give anything less than your best is to sacrifice the gift."
-Steve Prefontaine

Quarterback John Beck receiving running tips from 1996 Olympic gold medalist Dan O'Brien. (Chapter 48).

Growing up, John Beck was a small, skinny kid with red hair. When I say small, I mean small. His 5'4" frame and 110 pounds did little to lend themselves to a successful little league athletics career. With size 13 feet, he more closely resembled Krusty the Clown than a championship athlete. Despite his physical disadvantage, John seemed to have more sense of purpose than the other kids. Even though he was always the underdog, he always found a way to win.

Years later, Beck quarterbacked his junior high football team, which seemed like one more losing proposition. His predecessor was Drew Henson, a remarkably talented athlete who later played baseball for the New York Yankees and quarterbacked for the Dallas Cowboys. Drew set all kinds of junior high records and no one associated with the program was excited about little John taking the helm. When all was said and done though, John found a way to lead his team to the championship and break Henson's records. The skinny little guy with purpose had once again emerged as an unlikely victor.

When he graduated from junior high, one of John's coaches told him, "I'm glad you had the chance to be a successful quarterback, because you'll never be good enough to play the position in high school." John disagreed. He knew he wanted to be quarterback at the perennial Arizona powerhouse Mountain View High School, and so he trained, and trained, and trained. He trained with that sense of purpose that John Beck always trained with.

John played junior varsity throughout his sophomore year. In the summer after his junior year, John went to the Stanford Football camp. Conducted by Stanford University coaches, the program draws high school players from all over the country. It gives high school kids the chance to learn from accomplished college coaches, and in turn, gives coaches exposure to athletes who may be talented enough for recruitment. At this camp, John received a report card which rated him in several categories, including leadership, arm strength, passing accuracy, coachability, and the potential to play football after high school graduation. John did not care for most of his grades, nor the critique that he was not a major college football prospect. In fact, he stormed into the head coach's office at Stanford University and told him he didn't like the evaluation grades. He told the coach he would outwork everyone and have a standout senior season. Keep in mind that this came from a quarterback who was going into his senior year without having thrown a single pass as quarterback for a high school team.

To make a long story short, John returned home from the Stanford Camp to start his first game as quarterback. His team was crushed and flat out embarrassed at almost every phase of the game. Still, John remained determined.

His team rebounded to win all of the other games that season, including a blowout win for the state championship. Apparently almost everyone except John underestimated his tenacity of purpose.

Even after this amazing season and improbable finish, the doubters persisted. John was not highly recruited to play college football. He had some prospects at junior colleges, but as the Stanford staff suggested, big time offers were noticeably absent.

As planned, John followed high school with a two year mission for the Mormon Church. Stationed in Portugal, it seemed unlikely he would play another down of football in his life. Undaunted, John ran hills, lifted weights, and threw footballs whenever time permitted, despite serving his church twelve to fifteen hours per day.

I had trained John before his mission, and when he returned I was afraid to find him plagued with inability and self-doubt. To my pleasure, he came back as John Beck, the same John Beck I had known. His sense of purpose had not changed. All totaled, he had played one high school season in the last five years, and hadn't even been on American soil for the last two years. Regardless, he wanted to be a great quarterback, and he had the will to make it happen.

After months of training, John chose to attend Brigham Young University. He wanted to be a standout quarterback, a lofty aspiration to anyone who has ever seen a Brigham Young football game. The university's previous quarterbacks included Jim McMahon, Robbie Bosco, Ty Detmer, Steve Sargisian, and a host of other record-setting, nationally-acclaimed, All-American quarterbacks. Young and McMahon even went on to become quarterback Super Bowl winners. Brigham Young University is known for its record-setting quarterbacks, not for letting guys who have played one year of high school football over the last five calendar years run the ship.

John Beck made the team at BYU, but the team struggled his freshman year. Critics again doubted John. Four years later when he graduated, he was second on the school's all-time leading passers list. His final college statistics surpassed both Super Bowl Champion quarterbacks, Young and McMahon, and John led them to an 11-2 record with a bowl victory and a number fifteen national ranking. One can only imagine what he might have done with the talent of perennial powerhouses like Notre Dame, Michigan or USC. Shortly after his college career ended, he found himself starting games as a rookie quarterback for the Miami Dolphins.

I don't think John Beck was born to be a quarterback. I think he merely has a solid sense of purpose that guides him in all of his endeavors. John Beck is a devout member of his church, a loving husband to his wife Barb, a great father, and a quarterback who is always questioned but always emerges the unlikely victor. Don't bet against John Beck. He's proven, over and over again, the power of having a sense of purpose.

Chapter 12

LOYALTY AND LOVE
HERSHEY AND JANET

"The greatest thing you will ever learn is just to love and be loved in return."
-Eden Ahbez, from the hit song, "Nature Boy"

I am probably heading into a great deal of trouble by likening my late dog Hershey, a beautiful chocolate Labrador retriever, to my wife, Janet. Yet the shoe fits, so I'm going with it.

We've owned five Labradors to date, and though we've loved them all, something about Hershey was different. Mellow on the inside and a fun retriever on the outside, she had a sort of charisma that made everybody love her. Some of our friends liked White Dog for her enthusiasm for retrieval. Others were attracted to the goofiness and easygoing spirit of our big black lab, Jackie, who was nicknamed Knucklehound. Many like the sweetness of Geronimo, while others preferred the spirit of Musashi. While most seemed to have a definitive favorite, all seemed drawn to Hershey, as though by some magnetic field.

About five years before Hershey died of lung cancer, I joked to Janet, "Everyone loves you, just like every one loves Hershey." That was later shortened to, "Everyone loves Hershey and Janet." I said that in passing, but heard myself saying it more frequently as the months went by. I said it enough to be fascinated by it. Hershey was a different sort of dog: a happy, loyal, loving dog. At some point I realized I had hit the nail on the head. Janet and

Hershey were alike in so many ways.

I don't think a person in the world has ever disliked my wife Janet. Like Hershey, Janet is happy, wonderful, caring, and giving. She has a way of touching lives and touching people. Mellow at times, like Hershey, and outgoing and fun at times, like Hershey, she is someone you find yourself instantly attracted to. Everyone feels good around Janet. Everyone feels loved, and they love her in return.

Hershey and Janet: two peas in a pod for life.

Both Janet and Hershey are loyal and loving. Their love is unyielding and unwavering. There's a security and consistency in the love that I receive from my wife, and it is beyond the reach of mood or fluctuation. It is the same sort of love Hershey gave. If the huskies mentioned in Chapter 6 have every cell of their body programmed for running the sleds, Janet and Hershey seem to have all of their cells dedicated to providing loyalty and love. To her last days, when Hershey's cancer had ravaged her lungs, making it a struggle to breathe, she remained loyal and provided for her owners. I have a photograph of her with the newspaper from this time. She struggled to reach the end of the driveway but barked at the door each morning anyway, so we would give her the chance to retrieve it for us. She gave every bit that she had as her sign of love to us. It was her special task to get that paper for us, and she did it by her own choosing, right up until her life ended.

Likewise, Janet has had her struggles. While pursuing competency in judo and karate over the past fifteen years, she has had an unfortunate time with knee surgeries. She's had five of them. Despite this, she too has given me every bit that she had as a sign of her love. Once, the day after she had anterior

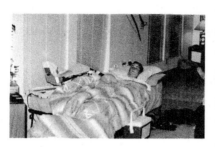 cruciate ligament (ACL) reconstruction, when she was in severe pain, she hobbled from the make-shift bed in the living room to the kitchen on crutches. I asked Janet if I could go get whatever it was she needed and she said, "I was going to see what I could prepare for you guys."

Janet has never been anything but this way to me and I already know, deep in my heart, with perfect certainty, she too will always express her loyalty and love to me, to our families, to our friends.

"Everyone loves Hershey and Janet." I am a lucky man to have learned from two beings, one canine and one human, who could not be topped as teachers when it comes to loyalty and love.

Chapter 13

ENTHUSIASM
STEPHANIE PREACH

"Every great and commanding movement in the annals of the world is the triumph of enthusiasm. Nothing great was ever achieved without it."
  -Ralph Waldo Emerson

I liked this kid the minute I met her. There was something different about her, something about her happiness, enthusiasm, and outgoingness. When I say kid, I literally mean a kid. Stephanie Preach was twelve when I met her. The youngest of four daughters, Stephanie would come watch her older sisters play volleyball. I met her at the high school games. What can an adult learn from a junior high student? In theory, the adult should provide the education and mentorship. But I am not ashamed to say that Stephanie Preach has taught me. Rather, I feel blessed that she has.

In one of my first memories of Stephanie, she was sitting at her older sister Lindsay's volleyball game. At the time, Lindsay's team, Xavier College Preparatory, was the top volleyball school in the highest division of volleyball in Arizona. Stephanie, only in eighth grade, played at Saint Jerome Middle School. Saint Jerome Middle School was far from being a volleyball powerhouse. Even as far as middle school volleyball teams go, Saint Jerome's program was below average.

"Steph, are you going to be ready to do this next year?" I asked, wondering if she had thought ahead about trying out for the freshman team at Xavier.

"I'm ready right now. I'm playing varsity next year," she said, with a definitive look in her eyes.

"Wow", I thought to myself. She's only in eighth grade, and in a pretty poor program. And when I ask her if she'll be ready to try out for a volleyball powerhouse's freshman team, she thinks she'll skip freshman and junior varsity programs and start at varsity level. I love the way this girl thinks. I heard no hesitation in her voice, just pure enthusiasm.

Stephanie Preach never played a minute of freshman or junior varsity volleyball. As she planned, she joined the varsity team. Even more unique, Stephanie didn't play as a setter on the varsity team, which was her position. Her older sister Kristin was the setter and a first team All-State selection herself, and so Stephanie had to make the team in a position other than her own—which she did, in spite of being undersized and without the years of training many of the other girls had.

Watching Stephanie play is like admiring a work of art. Stephanie Preach is so enthusiastic and passionate that her love for the game feeds the enthusiasm of her teammates and those rooting for her.

In the state playoffs her freshman year, a player on the opposite team pounded a hard ball that bounced off one of her teammates and headed deep out of bounds at the back end of court. In a mad dash, Stephanie somehow caught up to the ball, passed it back onto the court, and then crashed through double doors of some closet. She had obviously fallen down in that closet and, judging by the loud sounds, had taken a lot of equipment down with her.

How she made that perfect pass I'll never know, but I will always remember watching her burst back through the closet doors like some sort of superhero. A moment later, she dug the next shot and saved the point for Xavier—the same point they had been working on when she crashed through the closet doors. My words fall short in describing the enthusiasm, passion, and love of the game I see from Stephanie Preach every time she plays. Since a picture is worth a thousand words, I will allow them to do the talking.

Thank you, my young teacher, for showing this old coach the way everyone should play, the way everyone should approach life: with utmost enthusiasm. May you never change.

NO ORDINARY MOMENTS

KEVIN JACKSON

"Focus on the possibilities, not on the problems."
    -Anonymous

Kevin Jackson: Olympic gold medalist, Ultimate Fighting Champion, and Olympic team coach.

Dan Millman sure changed a lot of lives when he wrote the bestselling book, "Way of the Peaceful Warrior". For those who have not read it, I cannot recommend a book more highly. The book's premise is that a lost gymnast finds a mentor, whom he calls—very appropriately—Socrates. Socrates guides him in his search for the meaning of life, which the gymnast decides is this: "There are no ordinary moments." I take this to mean that we all have the power to create significance; we don't need to settle for the unmemorable, the ordinary.

I associate Kevin Jackson with that quote. He has had plenty of extraordinary moments. He is happily married, has beautiful children, and has been the head coach of the United States Olympic freestyle wrestling team.

As a competitive wrestler, he won the NCAA Championships, the Freestyle National Championships, the World Championships twice, and the Olympic Games. Indeed, he has had an atypical number of extraordinary moments.

Nevertheless, this is not why I think of Kevin and the peaceful warrior lifestyle hand-in-hand. The association came from one cold winter night many years ago. It was Sunday, at about ten at night, and my wife Janet and I had retired for the evening, since we usually get up before six. I had just fallen asleep when the phone rang.

"Tim, it's K. J. What are you dong?" he asked.

"I'm sleeping," I said. "Why?"

"I didn't get to train today."

I knew what this meant. Kevin Jackson is a really nice, happy, healthy and forthright man. Everyone in wrestling who knows Kevin Jackson loves him. I knew this was his way of telling me he wanted to train. At the time, he had just had a victory in the Freestyle World Cup Championships, and had been asked to fight for the World Championship belt in the Ultimate Fighting Championship. The event would take place three weeks later in Shin Yokahama, Japan.

I thought it was absurd. I love this guy, but does he really expect me to get out of bed at ten on a Sunday night to go fight? I thought this, but I already knew the answer. I was responsible for training him for this fight and he was a dear friend.

"I'll see you at 10:30," I said.

So it was. To Janet's disbelief, I climbed out of bed. I put on my protective cup, shorts, T-shirt, yards of tape and set out. I often marvel at how stupid I must have been that night. I had been in my bed, my comfortable bed, asleep. I got out of bed to fight a guy who had won multiple World Championships and Olympic Games, and who ranked as the number one mixed martial artist in the world. My friends have called me "more enthusiasm than intellect," and I suppose this is their proof.

The workout that night was a sort of blessing for me. We fought, and fought hard, for more than two hours. I was at the top of my game. I felt as though my judo and ju-jitsu technique were honed, and that even though Kevin was an Olympic champion wrestler, I was giving him an intense fight.

When we left at about half past midnight, I had this moment of regret. It had been fun, yes, but I would be beat up the next morning and would not get much sleep. I thought about how I would pay for this the entire next day.

We stepped out into the cool air and darkness surrounding my four-car garage, which had been converted into the dojo we just fought in. The moon hung, heavy and full, and brighter than usual. Something about the beauty of the shadows drove out the regret, and then Kevin said something I won't forget.

"These are the times you'll always remember. You never remember the ordinary moments."

I don't know if Kevin ever read "The Way of the Peaceful Warrior", but he seemed to have adopted the philosophy. Training with a dear friend like Kevin Jackson, who happens to be the two-time World Champion, Olympic champion, and number-one rated mixed martial arts fighter in the world, certainly qualifies as extraordinary. Coming out of that dojo, exhausted and drenched in sweat, and experiencing the beauty of the full moon and the crisp air was extraordinary. Getting a life lesson from a real-life Socrates was extraordinary.

Our days shouldn't be full of ordinary moments. We have so many opportunities to change the ordinary to the extraordinary, especially if we keep the peaceful warrior philosophy close. Kevin Jackson and Dan Millman together have taught me to create hundreds of extraordinary moments from ordinary circumstances. Thank you Dan Millman. Thank you Kevin Jackson, not for the beating you administered that night, but for uttering two lines from your heart that have enhanced the quality of my life. There need not be any ordinary moments.

Chapter 15

MY CHEAT SHEET
BILL ROBINSON

"Resolve to perform what you ought; perform without fail what you resolve."
-Benjamin Franklin

Bill, with daughters Jill (left) and Kerry (right) and wife Gloria

If there is a better man on earth than Bill Robinson, I'd like to meet him. Sure, that is a strong statement, but I'm sincere in saying that. Bill Robinson is just not your typical co-worker or ex-college roommate. I first met Bill when he was 74. Bill came to me to ask if I would help him with strength and conditioning. Not every 74 year old man walks into an elite athlete training center, past dozens of world class athletes, to ask if he too can be trained. But then again, Bill Robinson isn't a normal man. He's Bill Robinson.

When I met him, Bill was competing in tennis tournaments and swim meets. He struck me as sincere about wanting to train, and was charming, courteous, and funny. I figured I would give it a shot.

Before long, I found out that Bill and I live in different worlds. Bill likes fine arts, wine, and a night conversing with fellow intellects. I like martial arts, chicken and broccoli, and watching cage fights. Thankfully, we bonded anyway, and I want to share this story, which Bill told me about his childhood, and which captures his character.

At the age of fifteen, Bill came back from school particularly pleased one afternoon. As a self-proclaimed "scrawny Jewish kid," he earned his place as one of the high school's cheerleaders. He was thrilled, for the position gave him the chance to meet others, serve his school, and be involved in activities with other students. He was keen on getting home to tell his mother; this was one of the most significant achievements at that point in his life.

"Mom, I have something really important to tell you," he said.

"Bill, please sit down," his mother said. "I have something very important to tell you."

"But Mom, this is really important to me. I can't wait to tell you something."

"Bill, do you notice that we move every three months?"

"Yes, Mom. I do."

"Let me tell you why, Bill. This family is you and I, and only you and I. We get a new apartment, and I have to pay the last month's rent right away. Then I struggle to make the payment for the first month's rent. After the second month, I can't make rent payments at all. My salary isn't high enough. They evict us. You need to quit school and get a job. We have no chance of making it otherwise. There aren't many places left in Chicago. We have hit most of them."

So Bill dropped out of high school and looked for a job. Most businesses didn't want a fifteen-year-old (they wanted someone at least 16), and so Bill went days without finding work. As his mother became desperate, she told him to go to the Chicago Herald American office because they had a job opening in the advertising department. She told him to lie about his age, claim to be sixteen, and explain that he wanted to learn about advertising. If he didn't get a job soon they would be living in the street, and streets in old-time Chicago were not kind to women and children.

Bill went to the Chicago Herald American the next day, lied about his age, and sought employment in the advertising department. He was hired, and started his advertising career. As he became more versed in the advertising field, his job led to an interest and opportunity in marketing, which became his passion.

When Bill retired and ended his career, he did so from his own marketing company. The firm, based in Chicago, had grown to include branches in New York City and Los Angeles at times. Bill wrote ten books and two hundred magazine articles on marketing. He spoke on the subject in a variety of foreign countries, and became known worldwide as one of the tops in the profession. I'm astonished that his career stemmed from such humble beginnings.

After getting to know Bill Robinson, I know that such miracles are just part of what Bill Robinson can create. Bill has been married for over fifty years and has three children, all of whom went on to be successes in their own right. He donates freely to charities, and spends endless hours volunteering his time and expertise to organizations like the Phoenix Ballet. At 82 years old, this high school dropout still takes college classes every semester. He still trains with me, amongst many of the top athletes in professional sports. He knows everyone at the gym. He belongs to book clubs, movie clubs, and competitive swimming. On his 82nd birthday, because Bill was still so fit, I was able to give him a very special gift: the twenty pound weight vest he had to wear during the workout. This was an old Ja Shin Do idea, created by Andy Bauman. What better day to accomplish a difficult workout than your own birthday? Better yet, since Bill is the high-achieving man that he is, I put him in that vest twice that week.

There isn't anyone who knows Bill and doesn't love him. He has this way of caring about everyone, and helping them bring out their best. One thing I know for certain, no matter what it is that Bill Robinson attempts, he always does it right, and there is always resolution. With Bill Robinson, it just could not be any other way.

Although we came from different planets, I cherish the lessons I have learned from Bill Robinson. Without ever saying a word, he has made me vow to keep both my body and mind sharp for life. Through his example I hope to always achieve an acceptable level of resolution in all endeavors, in all areas throughout my life. Thank you, Bill, for being my "cheat sheet." I know, through your example, how to proceed through the rest of my life. All I have to do is follow your lead. Count on me to do so. I have learned from the best.

Chapter 16

HUMAN CAPABILITY

VASILLIY JIROV

"Cruel physical training cultivates a dauntless spirit. One can withstand any pain."

-From the martial art documentary, "Budo"

One afternoon in 2004, the phone rang and the man on the other end introduced himself in a thick Russian accent as Vasilliy Jirov, the current International Boxing Federation Cruiserweight World Champion. He wanted me to prepare him for his much-anticipated world title defense against seven-time World Champ James "Lights Out" Toney. I told Vasilliy I recognized him and had seen him fight. I added that I liked his fighting style and toughness,

and that I looked forward to training a man reputed to be an extraordinarily hard worker.

When Vasilliy arrived, we went through the customary question and answer period. I took notes on his medical history, strengths and weaknesses as a fighter, and training preferences. We went through preliminary pre-test measures to assess his physical state. Before he came to me, he wasn't sure when he would have his next fight. He had been hiking, but otherwise hadn't been training so he wasn't in great shape. We went right to business. I only had six weeks to prepare him for camp with legendary trainer Tommy Brooks. Vasilliy assured me he would do whatever I asked of him and whatever he needed to do to be ready for Tommy. I liked him right away. As I got to know him better, I found him to be tough as nails, dedicated, disciplined, focused, caring, friendly and funny.

Over those six weeks we progressed from entry-level workouts—designed for a boxer who had not been in good shape—to workouts that many professional athletes in the gym called inhumane. Toward the end, training involved high-intensity, full-body, boxing-specific strength and endurance training. Circuits combined high-repetition sets of power cleans, uphill treadmill runs, weighted vest split squat jumps, clapping push-ups, and all-out medicine ball throws. These circuits often lasted as long as seven minutes per round. Vasilliy usually  maintained his heart rate at two hundred beats per minute for six consecutive minutes. At one point, professional football player Fred Wakefield of the Arizona Cardinals, insisted that I stop. "This isn't something you are doing for him," he said. "This is something you are doing to him." And furthermore, "He could die from this." Indeed, I probably pushed him to the limits of human capacity. Vasilliy never slowed down and never complained. He attacked every bit of it.

One afternoon after yet another of these high intensity circuits, we sat down and talked. I explained to Vasilliy that I was sorry for making every minute of training a seemingly brutal test of his resolve and physical capacity. I told him this really wasn't my pleasure, but I had to administer the workouts I thought were right for him. After all, he was going to fight a beast nicknamed "Lights Out."

"Team," he said, referring to me in his heavy accent, "do whatever you have to do to me. I assure you I have had worse."

"Worse?" I thought. "How could he possibly have had worse?" I knew he told the truth because he was Vasilliy, and Vasilliy was full of integrity. I just couldn't figure out how he could possibly have had worse.

"Team, when I was in Russia I had this crazy coach who did much worse to me. He would row me out two miles into very cold lake and make me swim back. He locked me in long narrow hallway and released attack dogs at me. He would make me spar for hours. Believe me, Team, this was much worse."

"Vasilliy, I apologize. I'm not questioning your honesty, but did he really release attack dogs at you?" I asked.

"Yes Team," he said, without emotion. "Here are scars from dog bite. I have them in three places. Everyone said this man was crazy but I won the Olympic Games and also the outstanding boxer award. He helped me very much. It was all worth it."

Jirov versus Toney: the 2004 fight of the year. The animosity towards each other was so great neither fighter wanted to retreat to their stool at the bell.

I've reflected on this conversation many times over the past years, especially when I'm feeling adversity in my own training as a martial artist. It has often been said the greatest waste of all is the waste of human potential. Vasilliy's story made me realize how much potential is probably wasted. I often tell the story when athletes tell me I don't know how tired they are, or how difficult their training has been. In my thirty years of conditioning athletes, I've never heard of a training program that remotely approaches what Vasilliy had gone through. But then again, only one Olympic boxer can be a champion in his weight class. Only one Olympic boxer can be named the outstanding boxer for all weight classes. Only one professional can be the IBF World Champion. That one was Vasilliy Jirov, and the lesson he taught me about human capacity has served to strengthen me for the rest of my life. Thank you Vasilliy for being not only a gentleman and a friend, but also for being an inspiration as a warrior.

Chapter 17

LIFE'S FULL CIRCLE
WHITE DOG

"If wrinkles must be written upon our brows, let them not be written upon the heart. The spirit should not grow old."
    -James A. Garfield

In November of 1994, I asked my wife Janet for suggestions for her Christmas present. I love spending Christmas with Janet. Christmas brings out her inner child. We had talked about having dogs as pets, and had a running joke that we would get two Dobermans, a male and a female, and name them Napoleon and Josephine. Still, Janet surprised me by her request for an actual dog,

White Dog at five weeks old, the cutest puppy ever.

"a little yellow Labrador retriever puppy that is really white in color." I had not expected this, and I wasn't sure I wanted to change our lives in that way. With no pets and no kids we could come and go as we pleased. Puppies demand time and attention and I wasn't really ready for the commitment.

"How about a tennis bracelet?" I asked.

"No, but thank you," she said. "I'd really like the puppy."

Janet got her puppy on December 24th, the cutest little Labrador retriever ever. Fittingly, we named her, "White Dog." While White Dog was as cute as a puppy could be, and was indeed exactly what Janet asked for, a problem soon arose. White Dog attached herself to me. I'm still not sure how this happened, but in her eyes, the sun rose and set with her newfound daddy. It was not that way with Janet. It was as if Janet was White Dog's arch-nemesis.

Janet's relationship with young White Dog

My relationship with young White Dog

For my part, I found the dog's love quite endearing. It wasn't long before I had an awkward phone conversation, one that could have gotten me in big trouble with Janet. I had called her on the way home from work one night.

"Hi, I'm on my way home," I said.

"That's great," Janet said. "I'm looking forward to seeing you."

"How's my girl?" I asked.

"I'm really good," Janet said.

"Hmmm."

I must not have sounded that enthused because after a moment, Janet said,

"Hey! You're not asking about me. You're asking about the dog, aren't you?" I was indeed referring to White Dog as "my girl." The transformation had happened: Janet out, White Dog in. It became our joke for years, that Janet was my girl until White Dog came along. For some unknown reason, perhaps because we're both more enthusiasm than intellect, White Dog and I had a psychic bond of love from day one.

It is interesting to see dog owners and their interactions with their "best friends." Some people purchase dogs and chain them in the back yard with little or no interaction. I just don't see the point in this. In my eyes it is cruel to the dog and wastes the potential of a meaningful relationship between man and animal. Others establish relationships in which the dog is considered a vital member of the family and is treated as such. This is the approach that Janet and I have had.

It is this style of relationship that has enabled me to grow considerably from my years with White Dog. My family always had dogs when we were growing up, but I was so busy with sports I never had immediate responsibility of the well being of the animal. Quite frankly, I did not know what that responsibility would entail. As of Christmas 1994, however, I became co-responsible for the health, care, feeding, well-being, and actions of a living being that thought I was the greatest thing on earth.

I also thought she was something special, nothing short of brilliant. In fact, I saw her outsmart Janet on many occasions. Some nights, Janet would put the puppy out the bedroom door and the puppy would sneak back in the doggie door on the other side of the house. Janet would open up the bedroom door and yell for the dog, not realizing White Dog was standing behind her looking up at her as if wondering why this lunatic of a mother was yelling her name to an empty yard. Then there were the infamous Frisbee episodes, during which White Dog would retrieve for hours. When Janet would finally have had enough of throwing Frisbees for White Dog to retrieve, she would attempt to grab the Frisbee from White Dog's mouth. White Dog would run to the pool, drop the Frisbee, and push it down to the second step with her paw. She knew this was too far under water for Janet to reach, and that her Frisbee could not be taken away. Janet and I would laugh and laugh. Thankfully Janet was good natured about it all and would recognize when White Dog had her in check-mate. Despite her brilliance, I didn't anticipate learning lessons from a canine.

Much like Rachel, Kelly and Madison the husky, White Dog possessed intense passion. Her passion for retrieving was second to none. I remember the stories told to me by my friend about the competitive retrieval successes of his labs. After meeting and seeing White Dog retrieve for only half and hour, he said there was no comparison. He was shocked to see me hold a Frisbee

five feet away from White Dog while tapping her on the nose with an edible dog biscuit—only to see her push the biscuit out of the way so she had better vision to see and bark at the Frisbee. The Frisbee was that much more appealing to her than food. I have often said that when I find just one athlete to coach with that much desire, I will coach that athlete to success and then retire happily. This retrieval passion, however, is not the focus of this chapter. Rather, I want to focus on the care and love we gave to White Dog and the lesson we learned from her throughout her

life's full circle.

The early years were easy. We fed her good food, food that would nourish her, gave her lots of stimulation, and helped her pursue her passion for retrieving. We spent time every day throwing Frisbees, tennis balls, or sticks. We even had "Pro Pitcher Wednesday," at which time several professional baseball pitchers came over to work out and would throw objects to her for hours. In some ways,

I now see her life as a parallel to mine. Until my middle-age years, I needed the same things: nourishing food, stimulation, and to pursue my passions—which happened to be coaching athletes and learning martial arts. We were like each other—focused, passionate, driven, and energetic.

Life passes more quickly for dogs, and eleven years into White Dog's life she developed arthritis, an inability to sprint, slight clouds over the eyes, limping, and at times she preferred a belly rub to chasing down an old tennis ball. I realized then my life would parallel White Dog's. I would need to back off my obsessive pursuit of martial arts. I too would no longer have the physical tools that I once had in youth. I would probably be more susceptible to illness and would need more care. As our veterinarian said, "There comes a time when you need to find her a soft bed and make her happy". Is this any different than the life span of a human?

White Dog got her soft bed, but we kept her active with swimming. I applied my knowledge of the training of arthritic humans for her. We helped her to pursue her passion and maintain her health as best as we could, though the arthritis kept her from the chases we did on land. The swimming had been amazing for her, and she was truly happy, through the intense hours of chasing on land had become fifteen minutes of retrieving in the pool. Janet sang to her and White Dog sang back. White Dog's death may be the worst tragedy of my life. I believe she is now in doggie heaven, fully capable of retrieving far-tossed Frisbees for hours on end, the way her genes demanded of her. I saw her grow from three weeks old, young and lost, to energetic and driven, then mellow and sweet, and finally, ready to make the journey to heaven.

I would recommend every person raise a dog at some point during their life and to treat that dog like a member of the family. In doing so,with White Dog, I have had the blessing of seeing unparalleled passion. I have also seen what lies ahead in the future for Janet and I. We have vowed to eat good, nourishing food and to maintain an ideal body weight. We have vowed to exercise and pursue our passion, but to do so in reason. We view this as running a marathon, not merely running a sprint and then burning out. We have also vowed to seek intellectual stimulation to keep our brains sharp. We know there will be times we will need a soft bed to merely be comfortable. We also know the importance of acknowledging the help we have been given and by returning those favors with love. White Dog has helped to teach us these things. A one-time relentless retriever was given a chance for a great life, and in return gave us a chance for a greater life as well.

White Dog will forever be my blessed girl and my astute teacher. I hope she'll be ready to chase for a long time, because my version of heaven will be all of us in a huge back yard throwing her lots and lots of Frisbees.

Chapter 18

REACHING OUT TO OTHERS
STACY DRAGILA

"The unselfish effort to bring cheer to others will be the beginning of a happier life for ourselves."
-Helen Keller

Stacy (right) mentoring Sarah "Iron Child" Hedberg. Iron Child is one of the many lives Stacy has touched.

Stacy Dragila is a stunning woman. She has been blessed with a beautiful athletic body, which she has put countless hours of work into building, on tracks and in weightrooms all over the world. Her accolades include winning the Olympic gold medal in the pole vault, the Indoor and Outdoor World Championships, several National Championship titles and breaking about two dozen Olympic, World and National records. To complement her beauty, she is lively and positive. As my mother Jessica, then eighty, said after dinner with her, "Wow, she's the total package." I have to agree.

Stacy has followed my direction, regardless of the difficulty level, to perfection. She gives me nothing but her best efforts. She has been this way at times when she was breaking records and vaulting higher than she ever had before, and she has been this way in the down times, when she needed surgery from popping her Achilles tendon while running hurdles. I care a lot about Stacy as an athlete I train, and she knows, even when she is on the other side of the globe, that I will be there for her.

While her list of virtues is extensive, one stands out to me even more than her world domination, Olympic gold medal, or two dozen world and national records: her ability to reach out to others.

Being a world-class athlete seems like a lot of fun and glamour—glamour in the newscasts, over the internet, and in the magazines. But backstage, life is demanding and stressful. Athletes like Stacy train four intense hours a day, almost every day each year, in hopes of changing their best vault as little as one inch. The sport requires being on a diet almost every day for fifteen years. Reporters and critics take unjustified shots at them in worldwide media when they've never met or talked to the athletes.

Worse, an athlete can undergo all of this and then fail to perform well. I have seen athletes train for an entire year on a training protocol that produced spectacular results the year before, only to fail miserably. That is enough to confuse any athlete's mind. Sometimes, for these reasons, world-class athletes need to focus exclusively on themselves and their performance. Not enough time or energy exists to give to others.

Stacy Dragila is the exception to this rule. Sure, she trains like an animal, twice on most days, three on others. She gets beat up physically and beat down mentally, like many hard-driving athletes. She has highs that anyone would want to have and lows I wish on no one. In spite of this, I have seen her serve as friend, helper, and mentor. I have seen her give undivided attention to Kelly Williams and Rachel Loutus, two high-school underclassman pole vaulters with personal bests of under ten feet, only sixty percent of Stacy's best. Stacy treated them like the world's best. She asked volleyball player Kaitlin Mackay what she had eaten every day in a motherly attempt to ensure she had enough energy to get through her difficult workouts. She led our entire gym through abdominal workouts daily. Once, she even had a twelve-year-old girl, a cheerleader, stay with her for a week as part of a big-sister mentoring program. Even our chocolate Labrador Retriever, Geronimo, benefited from Stacy's long belly rubs. Perhaps most impressive, though, Stacy relentlessly trained April Steiner, an up-and-coming pole vaulter who would eventually make the 2008 Olympic Team, a feat Stacy herself had failed to accomplish. Stacy left no stones unturned in terms of giving out love.

I'm not sure how Stacy summoned up the time or energy to reach out to so many people during the peak of her career, but I know that if she can do it at the peak of her career, we all can.

Chapter 19

MENTAL GROWTH
DR. JUDD BIASIOTTO

"Nothing can stop the man with the right mental attitude from achieving his goal; nothing can help the man with the wrong mental attitude."
    -Thomas Jefferson

Many stories of Dr. Judd preceded him, and rightfully so. This guy is just flat out amazing, and is amazing for so many reasons. These stories were told to me by another amazing man, a powerlifter named Fred Glass. I met Fred Glass early in my powerlifting career, while I was still in college. At that time he had been through twenty years of competitive lifting and I was still a novice. Three of us packed into a tiny car twice a week and drove an hour to lift weights in Fred's home. There was a good reason there were only three of us. Sure, we could have fit another person in the car. But I don't think we could have fit another person in Fred's basement. Regardless, the long drive we would make, which would get us back to our college campus close to midnight, was well worth the trip.

With Fred's background of having won national championships and setting national records, we hung on his every word. When Fred thought something was great, which he rarely did, we naturally assumed it was great. Dr. Judd

Biasiotto's name was one that seemed to pop up at every workout and was considered to be great, according to Fred.

Dr. Judd came from Easton, Pennsylvania, and had met Fred when he started powerlifting. Judd had a Ph.D. in sports psychology and became a proficient powerlifter. He had a typical squat style, with his torso pitched forward, like World Champion Larry Pacifico. Dr. Judd could squat an impressive 550 pounds in the 132 pound weight class limit, bench press 300 pounds, and deadlift 525 pounds. That he did this as a drug-free lifter made the feat that much more impressive. Fred introduced us to Dr. Judd, who was as strong and down to earth as Fred promised. We talked about powerlifting, training routines, and how to best train other athletes at great length. The time always flew when talking to Dr. Judd.

Shortly thereafter, Dr. Judd's powerlifting career took a turn south. He needed a major back operation, a laminectomy, for severely herniated discs. His doctors warned him that this would end his competitive career. When a surgeon has to hack deep into the back, untangle a nerve wrapped around a herniated disc, narrow out the foramen and remove the protruding disc, it seems the patient will never squat or deadlift any amount of weight ever again.

A year after the surgery, we were all amazed to find that Judd was attempting squats and deadlifts again. Not long after that, when I was the national records chairman for the American Drug Free Powerlifting Association, I got a request to process new certified records for Dr. Judd Biasiotto. My mouth dropped. After surgery, after we thought he would never lift again, and without strength-inducing drugs, Dr. Judd squatted 603 pounds, bench pressed 320 pounds, and deadlifted 551 pounds. I struggled to imagine any drug-free powerlifter weighing only 131 pounds squatting 603 pounds in competition. For someone to do this after a laminectomy was unthinkable.

I hadn't spoken with Dr. Judd for some time, but after this, I called him.

"Alright, Judd, how did you do it?" I asked.

81

"It was pretty simple, Tim, I just had to change my squat style from Larry Pacifico's, more to Rickey Dale Crain's. Sure it was hard at first, but once I got it down I made it simple."

"Everyone in this sport bends over like Larry Pacifico," I said. "Changing to Crain's style from Pacifico's is next to impossible. There's more to it and I want to know what it is."

"What percentage of sports is mental?" he asked.

"I don't know, Judd. You can't measure it, but everyone seems to think it's eighty-five to ninety percent," I said.

"So if a sport is ninety percent mental, are you or your training partners spending ninety percent of your time training mentally? I'm sure you're not, but I am. I'm using hypnosis, biofeedback machines, psychic driving techniques, and a whole host of other cutting edge ideas. I train twice a day mentally, every day without fail. It is so mentally exhausting I often feel more wiped out from my mental training sessions than I do from my gym sessions, but I just broke the American Record by over fifty pounds in the squat, so it's worth it to me. Now when are you going to get me those certificates?"

I really wasn't sure, at that time, what biofeedback machines, psychic driving techniques or hypnosis sessions were. I did, however, clearly understand that this guy had somehow put over fifty pounds on his squat after a back surgery that was supposed to end his career. He also somehow changed his squat style, which in my mind was roughly equivalent to a right-handed major league baseball pitcher who won sixteen games showing up years later winning twenty-five games as a left-handed pitcher. Dr. Judd had pulled off the impossible, and we all knew it. I had images of him using witchcraft, voodoo, and other supernatural powers I had never heard of. I got those certificates to him real fast.

Dr. Judd and I maintained a close friendship for many years. One year, at the National Collegiate Powerlifting Championships, a lifter in the 220 pound class picked a weight far too heavy for his first squat attempt. He took the bar down but never moved it at all, not even one inch. The weight looked about fifty pounds too heavy. In competition, you cannot lower your weight, so if you start too heavy, you have to try that weight again or else something heavier. Missing all three attempts in a particular category disqualifies you from the competition. This poor sap had obviously chosen a weight far too heavy for him, and was stuck with it. The second attempt went about as well as the first; it crushed the lifter. After this attempt, Dr. Judd went to the lifter and talked to him for twenty to thirty seconds. To my utter disbelief the lifter made the weight that had twice crushed him, on his third and final attempt. When I asked about this, Dr. Judd said he had told the lifter he believed he was strong enough to make it. To this day I still don't believe the lifter was strong enough to make the lift, and I don't believe that's all Dr. Judd told him. Regardless, he made it.

Dr. Judd: from champion powerlifter to champion bodybuilder. Regardless of the endeavor, Dr. Judd always ends up a champion.

Since then, Dr. Judd won the WNPC World Bodybuilding Championship, as their oldest champion in history. This would be equivalent to our left handed pitcher, formerly a right handed pitcher, now winning the batting championship. Only Dr. Judd...

Dr. Judd showed me, beyond any shadow of a doubt, that athletes and humans in general, can drastically change their performance via mental exercises. That message was as strong as the man that sent it. Thank you Dr. Judd.

Chapter 20

LOVING CHERISHED ONES
RICH AURILIA

"What is done in love is done well."
    -Vincent Van Gogh

A million things could be said about Rich Aurilia. All of them are good. Rich is just an incredible guy. He is generous, courteous, calm, caring and thoughtful. He is coachable, hard working and respectful. He has played over a dozen seasons in major league baseball, starred in the World Series, been selected to the All-star game, and has earned the reputation of a veteran player who would help younger players to become winners. As former American League Rookie of the Year, Eric Hinske said, "He's Rich Aurilia. He is kind of a big deal." Major league scoreboards bear testament to this. I am honored to say that I have not only coached him, but that he is my friend.

I could say many positive things about Rich Aurilia, but the following story better illustrates the quality of man he is. It was the 2006 season and Rich played for the Cincinnati Reds. Before each season, I send the major league baseball players I coach away with an unusual incentive clause. My financial reward is tied directly to their performance. I am not paid well if they don't play well, but I earn monetary bonuses from them when they succeed.

With three games left in the season, Rich was hitting .297 with 67 RBIs. He caught fire in the third to the last game: he went three for five at the plate, with a three-run home run and three RBIs. All totaled, the five at bats, three hits, three RBIs and home run cost Rich $135 toward my incentive bonus. Because the Reds were out of the playoff picture, he did not play the last two games and he did not lower his average.

At the close of the season, I received a phone call from Ann Frederick, of Stretch to Win. Ann specializes in flexibility, and she has worked with Rich for the past decade. She and I were delighted with his outcome for the season, and I shared with her that Rich's last game cost him $135.

"Knowing Rich," I said, "he'll say he is more than happy to give me that money because his performance was so good."

"I bet he will," Ann said.

Later that week, Rich called me and wanted to talk about off-season training. When I mentioned the financial ramifications of that last big game, he said, "I'm more than happy to pay you that."

Ann and I were right; this is the quality of person we were fortunate to work with.

While there is a lesson in this, and many others from Rich Aurilia, the most striking lesson I have learned from him was actually on another occasion. One night, I went with my wife Janet, my assistants Scott and Liz, and a few others from our training center, to watch Rich's wife Raquel perform. Raquel Aurilia sings professionally, and Rich bought us tickets to see her as the warm-up act for B. B. King. Heading out of the Dodge Theatre that night, we stopped by the stand set up for Raquel to sign autographs. As we approached to draw her attention, Rich popped up out of nowhere, with the speed of an all-star shortstop. We congratulated Raquel and told her how much we loved her singing and Raquel thanked us repeatedly for coming. Rich, on the other hand, was glowing. I cannot imagine that any husband on earth, anywhere, anytime, could glow more than that. Here was a World Series star, an all-star shortstop, who had never shown half this emotion when talking about his own professional baseball achievements, glowing at the sight of his wife.

Seeing that love that Rich had for Raquel, the way her accomplishments thrilled him though they weren't as universally recognized as his own, is something I won't forget. I sat silent in my forty-five minute drive home that night, reflecting on this lesson I learned from Rich, on what it means to love cherished ones from the bottom of your heart the way Rich does. I wish everyone in this world could have seen that sight. I am grateful to have seen it. Thank you, Raquel and Rich, for being Raquel and Rich. You're amazing.

Rich Aurila: He really is a big deal both on and off the field.

Chapter 21

ACTION

KENNY MONDAY

"Until intelligent thought is linked with appropriate action and follow through, there is no real accomplishment."
-Unknown

One summer day in 1996, I arrived to train a group of wrestlers in preparation for the 1996 Olympic Games. The first person I noticed, at the far end of the gym, was Kenny Monday. This was no big surprise. Kenny had been an overachiever all of his life, and he arrived early for training as a matter of routine. I am sure wrestling coaches all over the country have similar stories about Kenny Monday showing up early.

This was the first strength training workout we would have after Kenny won the 1996 Olympic Trials. It was quite a story. Kenny had won the Olympic gold medal in 1988 and was recognized

The great Kenny Monday receiving his mixed martial arts World Championship belt.

by many as the top wrestler in the world, regardless of weight class. Three days prior to competing in the 1992 Olympics, he dislocated his elbow and was told he should not wrestle. Against medical counsel, he wrestled and didn't give up a single point until his over-time loss to Jang-Soon Park of Korea in the gold medal match. It's hard to picture, in a sport with unparalleled depth of talent, that a guy could wrestle the whole Olympic tournament using one arm, and give up only one point. Kenny Monday was that kind of competitor, and that good of a technician.

After those 1992 Olympics, Kenny retired from wrestling. Years later he decided to try a comeback, and against all odds to make his third Olympic appearance. Meeting Kenny Monday, and having the opportunity to train him in 1995 and 1996, was one of the most fortunate experiences I will have during my lifetime.

On the aforementioned morning, I walked through the gym with a huge smile to congratulate my dear friend for successfully making a comeback and winning the Olympic Trials. He approached me with a big smile. As he drew near he started fidgeting with a watch on his left wrist. I then reached out to shake his hand and he put the watch in my hand and said, "Thank you Tim, for all you have done for me. I want you to have my Olympic watch."

What can you say about a man that gives you his Olympic watch? I wish I could do it justice. Writing about it over a decade later still evokes the same response. It isn't the watch itself, it's the caring, the thoughtfulness, the giving and most important, the action.

Kenny Monday has impressed me on numerous occasions, in numerous ways. When he wrestled, he was the best in the world. He was one of the first competitors ever to enter into cage fighting, and he won the Extreme Fighting World Championship. He was a successful entrepreneur, owning a Subway franchise and the Monday Morning Coffee Shop. Most importantly, he was just an amazing friend. Despite all of these successes, the attribute that comes to the forefront of my mind when thinking about Kenny Monday is his ability to act, to act strongly, and to act quickly.

A simple example of this occurred during a routine conversation after practice one day in 1996 when the Sunkist Kids legendary wrestling team was training for the Olympic Trials. The group consisted of Olympic gold medalists Kenny Monday and Kevin Jackson; Olympic silver medalist Zeke Jones; World

Champion Melvin Douglas; and National Champions Townsend Saunder, Mark Coleman, John Fisher, Mike VanArsdale and Mark Kerr.

"Come on over here Tim," Kenny said to me. "We're discussing double leg takedowns. I just keep working it until it's done. That's the way I see it. How do you see it?"

That was Kenny Monday – action. He simply worked things until they were done, whether it was beating the best in the world in wrestling, mixed martial arts, starting up a business or giving thanks to a friend who had tried to help him. He worked them all until he was done.

It has been said that action separates men; it separates winners from losers. Kenny Monday made that very clear to me, without ever saying a word about it.

Chapter 22

RECIPROCITY
DAN LACOUTURE

"He that does good for good's sake seeks neither paradise or reward, but he is sure of both in the end."
-William Penn

After a NHL game, in which he both scored a goal and won a fight, "Lac" seemed more interested in being a good friend than telling us of his success.

My long-time friend Dan LaCouture plays professional hockey. Although he is quite capable of scoring goals, his primary responsibility is policing the opposing team, to make sure they aren't getting too rough or too dirty. Some folks call people with this duty the team's "fighter." Others call it the "bouncer" or the "goon." Regardless of the term, it's a difficult way to earn a paycheck. Not everyone comes home from their work day with the routine concussion or dozens of stitches in the face, but Dan LaCouture does.

I met Dan over a decade ago, when I spent a summer in Boston working with hockey players of all ages and levels. I trained Dan, an aspiring NHL player, and found him focused and coachable. He wanted to be the best player he could be and seemed willing to undergo any training to achieve that end, regardless of the pain. Malcolm Gladwell wrote a terrific book about intuition called "Blink.". He theorized it possible to accurately assess a person you've known for only a few seconds. I had that gut response to Dan LaCouture. In the time it took me to blink, I knew I liked him.

I often gave Dan extra exercises, above and beyond the protocol prescribed for each workout. At the end of one such workout, he mentioned that his back felt tight. I was headed for my lunch break, so I told him I could take a half an hour to stretch him, to help alleviate some of the pain. Afterward, he thanked me for the extra effort and said he felt much better.

Our fight training sessions ranged from Phoenix, Arizona to Boston, Massachusetts. The only constants were that we were both going hard and we both loved each other afterwards.

Dan and I continued this pattern for a couple weeks. I often asked him about his fights in the minor leagues and about how he could gain a competitive edge over others, to ensure a longer career. We talked about fighting strategy on-ice as it compared to the off-ice stuff that I had done for so many years. We decided to get together later in the evening, to get away from the gym a few times a week so I could show him things that might help him during the upcoming season.

Several weeks later, after a workout, Dan asked me if I had plans for the upcoming Fourth of July weekend. I said I hoped my wife Janet would fly out because she always wanted to see Cape Cod. As soon as I said "Cape Cod," Dan blurted out, "Wait right here," and got up and walked away. I had no idea where he was going. I didn't know if I had offended him or even if I had hurt him by stretching him a little too far. All I knew is that he got up rather abruptly, barked at me, and walked away. I waited as he had directed. He sure seemed a little bit steamed up, so it really caught me off guard.

About ten minutes later he came back and said, "Mac, I got you a house in Cape Cod for the weekend. My parents own a house there and usually go down every weekend, but I told them they couldn't go this weekend because I wanted you to have the house with Janet. I'll bring you the keys tomorrow."

A man of the utmost integrity, honesty and character, Dan LaCouture brought me the keys the next day. I was thrilled to tell Janet we had a house on the Cape for a three day weekend. She'd dreamed of seeing the Cape since childhood. Honestly, I felt a little guilty that Lac's parents, Bill and Dottie, didn't get to use their own home that weekend. After all, I had not given Dan all of the extra time, attention, care, and expertise with expectation of reward. Rather, I had done it because I found him an outstanding person.

Dan LaCouture became a very good NHL player. He also became a very dear friend, one I know will be a dear friend for life. At times, Dan has come all the way from Boston to Phoenix to train with me in the off-season, and Janet and I have been thrilled to put him up in our house. I felt great the day he was able to provide me the opportunity to take my wife to a place she had always wanted to see . And it feels even better, as per his lesson, to reciprocate, when he comes to stay with us. It really feels better to give than to receive.

Lessons from "goons": you never know where the lessons are going to come from, but keep your eyes and ears open. Some of the best lessons can come from some of the most unlikely places. Then again, perhaps it makes sense to reciprocate to goons.

Chapter 23

STAYING TRUE

RANDALL MCDANIEL

"Go home with the girl you took to the dance."
    -Unknown

1985 photo of aspiring football players Randall McDaniel and Skip McClendon with aspiring strength coach Tim McClellan.

Barry Sanders, Steve Young, Walter Peyton and Jim Brown are often mentioned as the greatest players in the history of the National Football League. Who is to say who is the best? Each had his claim to fame and noticeable accomplishments to merit a vote.

Perhaps one way to make that determination would be to investigate the number of appearances in the Pro-Bowl, the game in which the top stars in the NFL are selected to play based on their performance during the season. Better yet, perhaps the person who started the most number of Pro-Bowls should win. Best of all might be the player who started the most number of consecutive Pro-Bowls. After all, this would indicate the best of the best over a long period of time.

Fans of Steve Young, Jim Brown, Walter Peyton or others might be disappointed if this was the criteria used for selection of the greatest player of all time, because none of those players would win. The guy who would win, and arguably be named the best player in NFL history, is a guy named Randall McDaniel. Randall started an NFL record twelve consecutive Pro-Bowls from 1989 to 2000.

Twenty-five years have passed since I met Randall, a polite, shy kid who grew up in Agua Fria, Arizona. At the time, Randall was a freshman tight-end at Arizona State University. It was easy to see at the time that he was athletically gifted. It was even easier to see his character, integrity and care for others. Having grown up in a small, then economically-challenged community, Randall did not have had the financial resources of some of his teammates, but he was rich in other ways.

A year after our first meeting, Randall found himself listed fourth on the depth chart at tight end, which means he wasn't expected to contribute much on the field. Undaunted, he trained harder than ever, because, as he told me, he wanted to help out his team. I'll never forget this conversation with Randall, because most kids at that age look towards individual glory and Randall's first concern was the welfare of the group, not his individual accolades.

All-American guard Randall McDaniel #62 in the 1986 season.

A few freak injuries to the offensive guards made head coach Daryl Rogers desperate enough to give Randall a try at the position. Coach Rogers probably had no idea this move would create the best guard in the history of the game, and perhaps the best player in the history of the game. Although undersized at

94

that time, Randall had become freaky-strong and was an exceptional natural athlete, and he excelled on the field.

1986 Drug-Free Collegiate National Powerlifting Champion Randall McDaniel photographed by *Powerlifting USA* editor Mike Lambert.

Shortly thereafter, I made plans to host the 1986 American Drug-Free Powerlifting Association's National Collegiate Championships. Arizona State was the defending National Championship team, and Randall asked me if he could lift at Nationals.

"Randall, you're a starting player now and you'd be risking injury lifting that heavy. The meet is right before spring ball. Are you sure you want to do this?" I asked.

"Yes. I think it would be fun and I want to help you guys win," he said.

Help us win... Once again, Randall thought of others first, even though it was already obvious he would have an extraordinary future as a football player. His character overshadowed his tremendous athleticism.

Help us out, he did. He squatted the collegiate national record, 640 pounds, and went on to win the individual national championship. The team points he earned helped Arizona State University to defend the title against the United States Air Force team.

The next two years went well for Randall, and he earned All-American honors and became the first found draft pick of the Minnesota Vikings. About that time I received a heart-felt letter of thanks from Randall and the woman who is now his wife, Marianne. Although I've coached dozens of first round picks in the last thirty years, his is the only handwritten letter of thanks I've ever received.

Randall's career took him to Minnesota, and mine kept me busy seventy to ninety hours a week. We lost touch. It wasn't until twelve years later that a good friend of mine, Penny Halling, mentioned to me that Randall regularly came to her clinic for physical therapy.

I always had a spot in my heart for Randall because of his character, coachability, and humble beginning. As I drove to Penny's clinic I wondered how twelve Pro-Bowls and having been named the best lineman in the history of the game might have changed him.

Randall hadn't changed one bit. He didn't look one day older and he didn't act one day older. I felt like I was a "Twilight Zone" episode, talking to

25 years later, still fit, still strong, still true.

the guy I had met seventeen years before. He asked me how I was and what I had done, listened well, told me about his own experiences, and was the same humble Randall. I think that was the only scenario I hadn't prepared myself for, and yet, after speaking to him I realized it was the only scenario that could have ever been. He was so strong in character, integrity, and humility that nothing could change him.

As if that wasn't enough, I recently received a voice mail from Randall, in which he announced that he would be inducted into the Pro Football Hall of Fame.

"Tim, this is Randall McDaniel. I wanted to make sure I had your correct mailing address. There were many people responsible for this Hall of Fame thing happening to me and you were a big part of that. I want to make sure you get invited to the ceremony."

Once again, by humbly suggesting that the Hall of Fame thing happened to him as a result of others' efforts, Randall showed his true self. By staying true to himself, he proved to be a Hall of Famer off the field as well as on it.

Randall's unique story does not stop there. Unlike many of his peers, Randall McDaniel is not a retired ex-player, living off the riches of his hard earned money. He serves as an educational assistant/tutor in a suburban Minneapolis elementary school, specializing in second grade teaching.

"Football was easy compared to this," McDaniel said of his new career. "It's good to give back and be that role model and give them something different to see. I like kids to get to know me as Mr. McDaniel, then find out later I played football. For young males, I read a lot with them. There are not many male role models in elementary school. Helping kids go down the right path is more rewarding."

Randall McDaniel, the hall of famer, stayed true to Randall McDaniel of very modest beginnings in Agua Fria, Arizona. Thankfully, he never let fame nor fortune change who he was on the inside. In remaining true to himself he has served as a role model for many, including me. And, as for going home with the girl he took to the dance, he and Marianne are still happily married.

Thank you Mr. McDaniel, my teacher.

Chapter 24

PEACEFUL WARRIOR
HANADA-SAN

"His smile can win even the hearts of little children; his anger can make a tiger crouch in fear. This succinctly describes the true martial artist."
 -Gichin Funakoshi, founder of Shotokan Karate

Dan Millman authored the best-selling book, "Way of the Peaceful Warrior." The notion of being both peaceful and a warrior has entranced me for the past fifteen years, since my friend Dave Vitagliano gave me the book as a gift.

The samurai warriors of feudal Japan and the monks of the Chinese Shaolin Temple serve as good historical examples of peaceful warriors. The samurai, in particular, are widely regarded as the best trained, most loyal, fiercest fighters in history. From the time they could walk, they were trained in all aspects of battle, both physically and psychologically. "Bushi damashi," the warrior spirit of ancient samurai, is a spirit unparalleled in the history of mankind. A warrior who performed poorly or with a hint of cowardice in battle could rectify his "disgrace" only by taking his own life. No other culture in history is as dedicated to the principals of loyalty, integrity, honesty, and good citizenship. Similarly, no culture trained its warriors so well for battle.

Though the warriors frequently fought to the death, their civilization did not want a collection of ruthless or lawless killers. Society mandated that samurai spend equal time training and performing more mellow tasks, such as writing poetry, playing music, writing calligraphy, or performing tea ceremonies. Deep immersion into such activity was supposed to create a harmonious balance, enabling the samurai to live properly. This is how I  understand the peaceful warrior to be, someone who is peaceful and gentle, but has the loyalty and strength to fight for a good cause.

I had my first real-life introduction to a peaceful warrior when I met Masaru Hanada, who is recognized as one of the greatest sumo wrestlers ever to live. That feat is monumental, given that Sumo wrestling dates back over fifteen hundred years. The crowning achievement amongst sumo wrestlers is the title Yokozuna (grand master). When Masaru Hanada retired, only sixty-seven sumos had earned that title in fifteen hundred years. Masaru Hanada, who fought under the name Wakanohana, was the sixty-sixth, and perhaps the most unlikely. Those who have a thorough knowledge of sumo would call him far too small to succeed at the sport, let alone earn the title of Yokozuna. Still, you can measure a man's biceps or his chest, but you cannot measure his heart. While Wakanohana was quite literally half the size of some of his opponents, his heart more than made up for it. Because of his unlikely yet consistent wins, he became the most popular Yokozuna in history.

Sumo is a brutal sport. Training of young sumos is so severe that many quit. That is the purpose of the training, to weed out everyone except the few who can withstand the pain. The sport itself is violent, producing more injuries than any other. In sumo, it is perfectly legal to charge off the line and thrust every ounce of your power through your hands into an opponent's throat. Too many times, the moving target, the throat, is missed and the result is a full-on palm strike to the opponent's nose, or a misplaced thumb rammed into the opponents eyeball. Deaths occur every year in sumo. The dietary regimen is vicious. Old time sumo stable masters (the sumo "coach") fed the younger sumos cold, often rancid food. As they achieved higher levels, they were entitled to have heated, non-rancid food. Because competitors seem to perform better at higher body weights, they must attain masses ranging from 400 to 650 pounds. Carrying all that mass alone can damage not only every joint, tendon, ligament in the body, but all of the internal organs as well. All totaled, sumo is a brutal endeavor. It is certainly not the place for someone who is undersized. Masaru Hanada withstood this lifestyle for thirty years.

I trained Hanada-san, as we called him, for a year. In that year he faced tremendous cultural differences; Japanese food, customs, rules, and etiquette are wildly different from our own. He spoke very little English. Still, for that year I never saw him without a smile. We made him do things he had never done before, like run two-hundred meter sprints in hundred degree heat. Since sumos don't run at all, this was quite the stressor to him. Even so, he was quick with a smile, a smile that always seemed to turn into laughter. At times, he would start saying who knows what in Japanese—he was probably cussing at us—but it was always funny. At times we worked him so hard he had to puke. When he'd return, though we never understood what he said, he'd make the scene so funny we would have tears in our eyes.

Hanada-san was exceptionally friendly, speaking (to the best of his ability) not only to the many professional athletes, but also to the younger high school kids in the program. At all times he practiced the humbleness befitting a warrior. He never mentioned his celebrity status or the Yokozuna title. He never seemed to think himself superior. He was gracious, caring, and he became one of us.

I feel privileged to have seen the peaceful side of one of the world's top warriors. Even without understanding half of what he said, I found this lifetime warrior every bit as funny as Jerry Seinfeld. In fact, at times we would have Japanese and American  people packed into our living room, and neither half really understood the other, but Hanada-san would have us all laughing until we ached.

To be blunt, I have been involved with sports my entire life, and I can be very unimpressed with much of it. I've met guys who are great at hitting fastballs but aren't particularly humble. I'm not impressed with people who have one God-given skill. The people I find impressive are those with tremendous character to compliment their skill.

Hanada-san is such a person. He achieved the virtually unachievable, as someone way undersized in the sport of giants. He went through the brutality of the training, the rancid food, and the injuries for nearly three decades. More important, he excelled equally out of the sumo ring as a humble man, friend, businessman, and one who likes to reach out to others. I am fortunate to have learned the real-life lesson of the peaceful warrior through him.

Chapter 25

VOLUNTEERING FOR TOUGH TASKS
THE SUMOS

"To give in to pain is to compromise oneself. To push through it is to emerge."
-Moetzscje

In 1997 I trained a friend of mine, Kevin Jackson, who was pursuing a career in mixed martial arts. He was already a World Champion and Olympic gold medalist in freestyle wrestling. Now he hoped to win the Ultimate Fighting Championships (UFC). The UFC had just started to gain acceptance outside of the United States, and Kevin planned to compete in a show staged in Japan.

Since my wife Janet and I have done ju-jitsu, judo, and karate for many years, after the fight we decided to extend our stay and tour the birthplace of these ancient martial arts. Our good friend Takayuki Sudo lived there, and he volunteered to guide us through the difficult Japanese cities. He took us to shrines, castles, gardens, the electronics district, and famous sites like Mount Fuji. We made several trips to dojos, including the very first Judo dojo, the Kodokan. We saw a variety of karate schools and dojos that practiced kyudo (archery) and aikido (a gentler form of ju-jitsu.)

One morning, Taka managed to get us into a sumo stable, which does not ordinarily allow visitors. Taka taught us the appropriate etiquette: we were to remove our shoes, bow to the stable master and anyone else who approached us, sit on a tatami mat in anza—a seated, cross-legged posture—in which we would remain still and upright. There was to be no talking.

We entered, bowed, and took our positions as the training started. The experience seemed surreal. For years I had watched my all-time favorite movie, a documentary titled "Budo", which chronicled the philosophy and history of several Japanese arts, including sumo. The movie shows the ancient training practices, which apparently have not changed much in the 1500 years of sumo's existence. Right in front of us, the sumos performed those exact drills. I felt as though we were living in the movie as they threw and pushed each other all over the hard green clay floor.

About two hours into the practice, my back was killing me. I had been sitting in the same posture that whole time. The sumo wrestlers had started a practice that resembled the king-of-the-mountain game kids play in the United States. One sumo, a giant who seemed to be at least 6'3" and over four hundred pounds, stood at the center of the sumo ring. He pointed at one of the other sumos, who would attack by trying to throw him, knock him down, or push him out of the ring. After the giant disposed of a wrestler he would point at another one and the process would continue. After each bout, all of the sumos would yell something in Japanese and raise their hand as they walked toward the king, the giant.

Janet leaned over to me. "What do you think they are saying?" I was at a loss. First, she surprised me—she'd risked getting us kicked out by asking that question. Second, I was certain that after thirteen years of marriage she would know my Japanese was not that extensive, and that I wouldn't have a clue.

"I have no idea," I said, thinking that would be the end of a conversation we shouldn't be having anyway.

"Tim, I think the other guys are saying 'Pick me, pick me,' because they want to go fight the giant," she said.

"I don't think so. Why would they want to fight that beast?" I said, pointing out the obvious. Then I sat—in silence, thankfully—to consider Janet's theory. After ten minutes my curiosity got the better of me. Against all good judgment and the etiquette I'd learned, I leaned over and asked my buddy Taka what the sumos were saying.

"Pick me, pick me," he said, to my surprise. Instead of hanging back in the pack and remaining safe, they were demonstrating their courage by volunteering to battle the giant, the king of the hill.

Amusing at the time (though trying to stand up and walk after three hours of sitting in one position wasn't amusing at all), the experience blossomed into a life lesson for me. The sumos volunteered for a tougher path though it meant probable defeat, embarrassment, and possible serious injury. Giving their best meant more than emerging—as some athletes do—by padding records with victories earned by fighting only easy opponents. The sumos didn't just accept fighting the giant. They volunteered. These men, so different from myself in looks, size, and shape, taught me a tremendously valuable lesson by example. They never said a word to me but I understood their message loud and clear.

Chapter 26

EFFECTIVE TEACHING
SENSEI YUTAKA YAGUCHI

"Developing excellent communication skills is absolutely essential to effective leadership. The leader must be able to share knowledge and ideas to transmit a sense of urgency and enthusiasm to others. If a leader can't get a message across clearly and motivate others to act on it, then having a message doesn't even matter."

-Gilbert Amelio, President and CEO of National Semiconductor Corp.

Sensei Yaguchi awarding the championship trophy to Jihone Du at the 2008 Shiai tournament.

In the previous chapter I mentioned that the sumos (who probably did not know a word of English) taught me a valuable life lesson without ever speaking to me. Sensei Yaguchi, against all odds, topped the sumos. The lesson I learned during my one and only training session with Sensei Yaguchi was not only noteworthy, but changed my perception about teaching, coaching, communicating, and leading to this very day.

By 2003, I had been in karate for almost two decades, and also studied judo, ju-jitsu, and a Russian martial art called Sombo. At the time, I was preparing for my black belt exam in Shotokan karate. The panel of evaluators included

Shawn Sample, a fifth degree black belt; Chuck Coburn, my direct sensei and a sixth degree black belt; Sensei Shojiro Koyama, a seventh degree black belt; and Sensei Yutaka Yaguchi, an eighth degree black belt. I was to be tested in basic fundamentals, kata—which are pre-arranged movement patterns, and free sparring ability. I felt no nervousness or pressure, just a sort of childlike enthusiasm. To be graded by these legends of Japan's original karate style seemed to me a once in a lifetime experience.

The test was scheduled for 8 p.m. on a Friday, in the ballroom of a hotel in Phoenix. Sensei Yaguchi, the honored guest, taught an hour and a half clinic just beforehand. Though the black belt exam would be demanding, it would be bad etiquette to disrespect a master clinician by not attending his clinic. So, I went.

Sensei Yaguchi taught a challenging clinic, during which he altered the technique of a hundred or so participants without ever saying a word. As one of the participants whose form he corrected, I can say that my karate skills improved that night.

Sensei Yaguchi stood in front of the room, calm, humble, and confident. He seemed to generate a sort of electricity, and every one of those hundred or so people paid complete attention. He demonstrated techniques, from the fairly simple to the very complex. Then he would then nod his head and bow. On cue, we practiced the techniques to the best of our ability.

I held out a punch at the end of one particularly difficult combination, a combination I thought I had performed fairly well, given the difficulty. Sensei Yaguchi walked up in front of me and bent down and stared at my fist as if to say, "Tim, the fist you have made is incorrect. The position of your first two fingers is not tight enough. Do a better job of flexing the distal knuckles and this will tighten your fist into what is appropriate. Do you understand this?" Fact is, he never said a word. After staring at my fist, he looked into my eyes. He had said nothing, yet he had said so much. I tightened my fist into a more acceptable position. He gave me a slight smile, his way of letting me know I had made the appropriate changes.

Before long I noticed he was changing some sort of mechanical error on every person in the room, some—like mine—very minor, and some huge. I often struggle to explain these sort of changes to students, even though I will try to explain several different ways, in a language we both understand. Even when I can convey the change I want, getting students to change their mechanics when their subconscious minds want to perform the improper motor skill can be challenging. I think every instructor in the world has struggled with this, and to see Sensei Yaguchi change a whole room without uttering a word defies logic to this day. He did so for over an hour without uttering one word.

Sensei Yaguchi is a master of karate-do. His fifty-plus years of performing this one art daily have given him extraordinary skills. But he impressed me more with his ability to lead, teach, and communicate. Never once did he yell. Never once did he berate. He simply made everyone better.

I think of this each time I watch a football practice and hear the excessive yelling at and berating of players. I think about this night when I am frustrated and have tried three, maybe four ways to get a martial arts student to change mechanics. I hope to have adopted just a little bit of Sensei Yaguchi's teaching style.

I am honored to have been recognized into the rank of black belt by this panel of legends. I am honored to have their approval and acknowledgement, but the accomplishment seems trivial compared to the lesson I learned from Sensei Yaguchi: the lesson of effective teaching. Thank you Sensei. May our paths meet again. Domo arigato gozai mashita. (Thank you very much.)

Chapter 27

RIDE OUT THE ROLLER COASTER

BILL SCHMIDT

"I have had nightmares and I have had dreams. It is because of the dreams that I can live through the nightmares."
  -Jonas Salk

Bill Schmidt winning the 1988 Drug-Free World Championships in Reading, England.

Bill Schmidt was my best childhood friend, all the way from elementary school through high school. He was the best man at my wedding, and I was the best man at his. Growing up, he was always honest, kind, smart, well-disciplined and just a wonderful person to be around. He was the type of person who exemplified what an eagle scout should be.

Bill and I often played sports together as we grew up. It was during our junior year, Coach Filipovits implemented a strength training program for us at Parkland High School. Bill had not played football that year, but decided that he missed the sport. He decided to lift weights to get bigger so he could play his senior year. I was excited by the possibility of playing with Bill again. Bill couldn't have played that junior year because he weighed only 120 pounds. There just isn't a spot on the football team for high school juniors who weigh 120 pounds.

He and I lifted every day until our senior year, when Bill reached 165 pounds and became a quick, fast nose tackle. Because of his weight lifting success, he competed in the Pennsylvania State High School Powerlifting Championship meet. He broke the state record in the bench press, the deadlift, and the total, and was named the Outstanding Lifter pound for pound.

When he attended Penn State University, he decided to take up competitive powerlifting and he proceeded to break the state collegiate bench press record. Having graduated with a degree in meteorology, he moved to Raleigh, North Carolina, to forecast weather. The problems began then. Before that, I had been able to coach Bill, to watch his every contest, and monitor some of his workouts. With him in North Carolina and me in Pennsylvania, too many miles separated us to continue that pattern.

The first ever American Drug-Free Powerlifting Association National Championships were held in 1983, in Allentown, PA. Bill planned to compete in them, and he trained accordingly. On my end, I sent him programs. He followed them, and astounded me with his successes during our phone conversations. He lifted heavier and heavier weights, especially in squats. In the workout before the meet, he told me he easily squatted 600 pounds three times, and felt certain he would squat close to 700. I wondered what they fed him in North Carolina. Bill used to squat 605 in competition, and as a drug free powerlifter, the improvement from 605 to the potential 700 boggled my mind.

I soon found out how he managed to squat so much. I found out during his warm-ups, just before the meet. As I watched Bill I realized he was squatting some nine inches higher than he needed to squat during the contest. Because he didn't go down as far he could take a lot more weight. He must have squatted higher and higher every week without realizing. That day marked a low in Bill Schmidt's powerlifting career. He wanted to squat 700 pounds, but even after we lowered his opening attempts to 589, he couldn't squat deep enough. It took him three tries to get that lift passed, and his finish was as miserable as his squats.

With proper supervision of his training partners, Bill climbed from the bottom of the roller coaster ride to the top by 1984. He lifted so well at the 1984 National Championships that we calculated he might make a 1,642 total, putting him in the highest category of "elite" total that a lifter could make. Few drug-free lifters in the world make the elite level. At that meet, the deadlift bar was

181 pound Bill Schmidt deadlifting 655 pounds in the dark, as only he would.

loaded to 655, which he needed to achieve his dream total and elite status. Just as the announcer called his name, the lights in the Holiday Inn ballroom went dim, apparently of a power shortage. Without hesitation, Bill ran in a dead sprint, leapt onto the stage, and in the dark, pulled the 655 pound deadlift. The judges told him to set the bar down, like a regular lift, which he did. The place erupted in a standing ovation. I think any other lifter that day would have complained about the power outage, and never attempted the lift, but not Bill. He was on the top of the roller coaster, and he knew nothing would stop him.

In 1985, the rollercoaster changed direction. He should have won the National Championships with ease, but his lifts were significantly lower. His squat was lower than the previous year. So was his bench lift. And his deadlift. All totaled, Bill struggled even to make one of each of his three lifts to achieve a total. He felt the bitter disappointment of an athlete who had shone just a year before.

In 1986 and 1987 he was amazing once again, winning the National Championships in San Jose and Chicago, qualifying him to compete for the United States team in the 1988 World Championships. The meet was held in Reading, England. Seeing his own photograph on a meet poster in Reading may well have been one of the highlights of his and my life. Bill Schmidt won those World Championships. His roller coaster ride had continued, and now he sat at the top, looking down.

At that time, Bill went through an unfortunate divorce. He worked out with less frequency and his weight ballooned up to 230 pounds. He became an ex-powerlifter, rapidly achieving high levels of cholesterol and blood pressure. Ten years passed with no sign of Bill Schmidt anywhere near the competitive platform.

As always, Bill Schmidt hit his low and then started to climb again. He started lifting in small North Carolina meets with marginal success. He never let the struggle get him down; he had been up and down so many times that he knew the drill. Three years later, he made the competitive bench press of 462 pounds, far better than the best he had ever done in his prime. The roller coaster took him to the top again, and this weight was almost a full 70 pounds better than his lifetime best. Sadly, a decline in performance followed during the next couple of years. As has always been the case, he once again rose to the top, establishing new Masters National records and winning the National Championship in 2009.

It has been said that champions get up one more time than they get knocked down. Bill Schmidt is indeed a champion and inspiration. May his successes remind us all to keep riding the roller coaster. Only in this way can we get back to the top.

An "up time" (left). Bill Schmidt on the podium's top spot at the World Championships.

A "down time". Bill missing a deadlift he should have made.

▲

Chapter 28

CRITICAL SELF-EVALUATION
RICK "THE JET" ROUFUS

"I tell you that as long as I can conceive something better than myself, I cannot rest easy unless I am striving to bring it in to existence."
  -George Bernard Shaw

Rick "The Jet" Roufus is one of the best kick boxers in the history of the United States. He won world championship titles six times in a career of more than sixty-five fights. He earned his nickname because his kicks and punches take off with the speed and power of a jet. In the heat of battle he lets his hands fly, and makes the fighting look beautiful, like the art that it is.

Rick's career hit big in the 1980s. Televised bouts showed him as this fast, tough, young, skillful fighter who could knock a man out, cold as a mackerel, with hand or foot. He continued his display of dazzling skill and athleticism all throughout the 1990s, winning World Championship after World Championship, in different weight classes. During this decade, Rick traveled the world, and fought and beat just about any man worthy of climbing in the ring with him. ESPN TV still shows some of his classic bouts, and he seems invincible.

Sadly, kickboxing's rising popularity took a turn south in the late 1990s. Boxing's popularity had grown with Mike Tyson, Evander Holyfield, and Lennox Lewis's bouts. Mixed martial arts, like the Ultimate Fighting Championships, began gaining public acceptance and growing fan bases. Simply put, kickboxing found itself squeezed out, and as the saying goes, "Warriors need wars."

Throughout this time, aging Rick Roufus continued training hard to maintain his skill. I met Rick around this time. He called me seeking strength and conditioning advice. When he called, I was in the gym training Siarhei Liakhovich, former Olympic and heavyweight boxing contender from Belarus. "Tim, he is good," Siarhei said to me. "I mean real good, like best in world kick boxer." I agreed to meet Rick at his own gym, the Roufus Kickboxing Center, in Tempe, Arizona, the following day. Rick hoped to be fit enough to compete in Japan, where kick boxing matches are still popular.

Photos of his historic battles hung from the walls in his dojo. The photo of him punching six-hundred pound sumo wrestler Akebono etched itself in my mind permanently. That a two-hundred pound person had enough faith in his skill to fight a gladiator three times his size stuck with me.

As someone who has kicked and punched for the last two decades, I had a deep appreciation for the way he hit bags and hand pads for his trainer, Carlos. He is, after all, The Jet, and his speed and power reflected that. The environment was electric. Music blared and twenty or so young, ripped, hungry fighters pounded away at bags and at each other - a martial artist's fantasy camp.

About forty-five minutes later, Carlos held the hand pads and asked Rick to do a difficult combination. Rick struggled with completing the task to his own or his trainer's satisfaction. Rick got angry, yelled, and stormed out the back door of his own gym. Of course, he returned a short time later, and then blew through that portion of the workout like a hurricane.

He probably seemed like a hot-headed and impatient man, pouting because he could not have his way. But to me, I saw a man who held himself to incredible standards, a man who evaluated himself honestly if harshly. He would not accept being good, very good, or even great. Rick Roufus had to be the very best he could be, and accepted nothing less. At that moment, I understood how Rick Roufus became one of the greatest kick boxers in the history of the United States.

Rick, thank you. Thank you for teaching me the need for accurate and critical self-evaluation. Thank you for showing me how this made you the best.

Chapter 29

PREPAREDNESS

SIARHEI "THE WHITE WOLF" LIAKHOVICH

"Before I get into the ring, I've already won or lost my fight out on the road. The real part is won or lost somewhere far away from the witnesses—behind the lines, in the gym and out of the road long before I dance under those lights."
-Muhammed Ali

This experience, to me, came right from a "Rocky" movie. I saw my first "Rocky" movie in high school, and it was fabulous. At that time, everyone in Allentown, Pennsylvania was talking about it. I imagine the rest of the country followed suit. I don't think anyone could have guessed this movie would spawn five sequels, the last of which would come twenty years later and feature the once young Sylvester Stallone approaching 60 years of age. The series had the potential to reach people at many levels and had the underdog theme, along with prejudice, patriotism, hi-tech training, will over skill training, hardship, a crazy old coach, the impossible upset, and the "Eye of the Tiger" all wrapped up in one.

I lived the "Rocky" movie. The story was a bit different than Sylvester Stallone's version, but I lived all of the aforementioned elements and it only took me three years, as opposed to Rocky's twenty.

This all occurred after I met Siarhei Liakhovich. Siarhei, pronounced

"Ser-gay," is a heavyweight professional boxer from Belarus. Belarus is just west of Russia. Siarhei looked exactly as you might picture a Belarussian boxer. He was 6'4", 225 pounds, and stoical. He used only as many words as were necessary and rarely showed emotion. I met Siarhei in 2004, through my trainee, IBF World Cruiserweight Champion, Vassiliy Jirov. Vassiliy had known Siarhei from their years of international experience as amateurs. They had attended camps and tournaments together, and both lived in Scottsdale, Arizona.

Siarhei started his professional career with sixteen consecutive victories. He then suffered a stunning upset to Maurice Harris, a fighter Siarhei was expected to beat.

Immediately after, he teamed up with legendary trainer, Kenny Weldon, who had coached more than twenty world champions.

Siarhei's year in 2004 went well under the guidance of Kenny Weldon and his new strength and conditioning program. Siarhei gained fifteen pounds without losing any speed or range of motion. This is critical for Siarhei's game, since heavyweight competitors seem to get larger every year. Siarhei won all of his fights that year, the culmination of which was a huge, nationally televised victory over Dominick Guinn. Dominick was thought to be America's next up and coming superstar, and so this defeat was Siarhei's finest hour. Siarhei had established himself as a legitimate heavyweight contender; few remembered he had lost to Maurice Harris.

By 2005, he was at the top of his game. He was ready to take on the world. Unfortunately, the world was not ready for Siarhei. His contenders knew he was on a roll and that he was a dangerous man. They did not want to fight him. Champions wouldn't fight him either, because he had a loss on his record and his world ranking wasn't high enough to merit a huge payday from promoters. You would think this would frustrate Siarhei, but he never let it get him down. He never changed his training. He trained with me four days a week for two and a half hours a day. He lifted weights until he could barely move. He ran until he could barely breathe. He hiked, stretched, did yoga, and swam. He never let up on his training.

At the height of his frustration, Siarhei signed with Don King Promotions. He was told he would fight Chris Byrd, the World Champion, in about two months. After twelve months of not fighting, many boxers wouldn't have been prepared for the rigors of an eight-week training camp. Siarhei was. He was prepared because he had never stopped training. My business partner Warren Anderson says, "the best way to get in shape is to never get out of shape." Siarhei was proof of this. He was absolutely ready to enter camp with Kenny Weldon.

Siarhei during a training session with Kenny Weldon.

The Chris Byrd fight never materialized because of a contractual disagreement that had nothing to do with Siarhei. Again, Siarhei was left without a fight. And again, instead of giving up, he trained as if he was signed to fight for the World Championship. Before we knew it, Don King called him. He would be fighting Lamon Brewster, the WBO World Champion, for his title. Siarhei hadn't fought in 16 months, but because of his preparedness, he was ready to go through the camp Kenny Weldon needed him to get through to be ready for this beast, Lamon Brewster. After all, this was Siarhei's chance to fulfill the dream he'd worked for, for eighteen years. Lamon Brewster had had fought thirty-three professional fights and had knocked out twenty-nine of those opponents. It was said he could knock down a building with his left hook.

It was finally fight time at the Wohlstein Center in Cleveland, Ohio. This was the main event. The lights were dimmed and Siarhei, Kenny, Ivalo Gotzev—Siarhei's manager and I entered the arena through a corridor of screaming fans. Unfortunately, the fans screamed at Siarhei, not for Siarhei. This was Cleveland. This was the United States and a predominantly African-American crowd. This was a crowd that was rooting for the champ. Lamon Brewster was that champ. Lamon Brewster was American. Lamon Brewster was African-American. Siarhei was the pale Belarussian and the contender. He was the bait for the shark.

The booing continued throughout most of the first half of the fight. Then Siarhei started to rock Lamon and the huge crowd started cheering for Siarhei instead. The whole thing seemed like a "Rocky" movie to me, until Brewster started rocking Siarhei. What a fight. The two warriors pounded away until the end of the twelfth round. With the crowd soundly behind Siarhei, Siarhei's hand was raised as the new WBO Heavyweight World Champion. Siarhei was able to fulfill his dream, even in spite of 2005, because he was always prepared. Being in that ring with Siarhei after the fight was as uplifting of an experience as a man can have, especially knowing everything Siarhei went through to achieve that.

Funny thing was on the way out, the fans who had booed him unmercifully on the way in were now yelling, "Champ, can I have an autograph? Champ, can I take a picture? Champ, you're the greatest!" It was like Rocky winning over the Russian crowd after his defeat of Ivan Drago, only in reverse. If those fans only knew what Siarhei had gone through.

Thank you Siarhei Liakhovich for following my direction, for working so hard, for being a living example of how an athlete should stay prepared, regardless of the ups and downs. Seeing a great person and good friend like you achieve a lifelong dream will forever be in my heart.

Chapter 30

GENEROSITY

MELISSA BUHL AND JOANNE GARCIA

"If there be any truer measure of a man than by what he does, it must be by what he gives."
  -Robert South

Joanne Garcia (left) and Melissa Buhl (right), seeming a real life "odd couple", share in the beauty of giving to others.

Joanne Garcia and Melissa Buhl are both objectively beautiful women, quick to smile, and well-liked. Both have been clients of mine for years, and so I know them well enough to know that they couldn't be more different. Joanne is middle-aged, happily married, and a mother of two. Melissa is half her age, single, and mothers only her two dogs. Joanne grew up cheerleading. Melissa grew up winning BMX races. Joanne trains for health and fitness. Melissa is a world-class professional downhill bicycle racer. Joanne goes to the salon on a regular basis. Melissa falls off her bike into the mud on a regular basis. The list goes on and on.

While similarities might be hard to find amongst these two clients of mine, they do have one trait in common. Both have been extremely gracious in showing appreciation for my services. They have shown gratitude with verbal thanks, E-mails, text messages, and monetary tips, more so than I have ever received from any other client. I have never received a check from either one of them as payment without extra tip money added, not in all the years I have coached both of them. This leaves me with a warm feeling and fondness in my heart for them. This sets them apart from anyone I have coached in the many years I have done so.

The beautiful middle-aged woman with the immaculate appearance and the dirt bike racer who won the world championships, national championships, and world cup championships all in the same year, may serve as a real-life odd couple, but both are my friends and teachers. Thank you Joanne for being the one and only Joanne. Thank you Melissa for being the one and only Melissa. You two have improved my life forever. You are so far from each other in many ways, but you share an expression of gratitude through generosity. You have taught me to show appreciation to others, above and beyond expectation.

▲

Chapter 31

PERFORMING YOUR ROLE
GREG HULL

"Tennis moms. I hate tennis moms. No positive change has ever occurred for a young player as a result of a tennis mom interfering with a coach's duty."
  -Unnamed local tennis coach

After a decade of competing in various track and field events, Greg Hull took up coaching. Over three decades later, he is still at it. His resume is impressive. He coached at two high schools and had stints at Scottsdale Community College, Long Beach State, Northern Arizona University and Arizona State University. Young athletes he coached won the United States High School Championships and two USA Junior National Championships. Later, he coached both men and women Olympic gold medalists in the pole vault and also two women's American record holders. He has coached even the most difficult athletes, athletes I would never have tolerated. I've witnessed it. Greg is a total package: he knows everything there is to know about the pole vault and has a gift for sharing that knowledge. I often take him to lunch to pick his brain about how he approaches training athletes.

Seven years ago he asked me to serve as a strength and conditioning coach for his most prized possession, his daughter Lindsay. Lindsay was an undersized thirteen-year-old aspiring volleyball player. Unfortunately, she didn't appear to have the height or special genetic gifts to become a successful high school player, let alone a college athlete.

After seven years and countless hours of painful workouts, Lindsay accomplished what seemed impossible. She had a standout high school career. She spiked; she dug; she passed; she did it all for her team. Still considered too short for good high school volleyball, she was recruited to play at a prestigious liberal arts college, Claremont McKenna. During her sophomore season she was named the team's most valuable player; during her junior year she became team captain. When her career concluded, she was recognized as one of the best players in the history of the school.

Lindsay Hull's level of determination far exceeds most athletes. For seven years I have put her through unbelievable workouts. She's passed out; she's puked; she's gotten her legs so full of lactic acid she's fallen down, unable to stand. We've done conventional training methods and very improvised ones. What this girl accomplished because of her determination, dedication, and extreme training methods could be a book in itself.

This chapter, however, is about her dad, Greg. He is a guy who has probably forgotten more about training than most coaches will ever learn. He is also a dad who never once said a word to me about how his daughter needed to be trained. That's saying a lot. I've had mothers with no exercise science degree, no certifications, and no coaching experience come in to tell me that their thirteen-year-old novice daughter needs to work such-and-such muscle group because that will help her volleyball serve the most. Then I have a coach of Olympic champions and American record holders who has never uttered a word. Seven years, not one word.

Greg knows full well I put Lindsey through things that bordered on inhumane. He knows about the times she got sick. He knows she was undersized for her sport. Greg also knows that coaches should coach, officials should officiate, and fathers should father. The whole system works best if everyone performs their own role. I coached and Greg permitted me to coach. There was no cross-contamination, as there almost always is in these endeavors—fathers yelling at coaches, kids second guessing referees, the proverbial soccer mom telling the coach what to do. I'm sure it had to be tough for him to stand back. I just found it so ironic that the only dad I've met who was qualified to provide advice to me never stepped in my way. It astounds me.

Lindsay had unbelievable determination. Greg had trust. They both performed their roles to perfection: Greg as the father, Lindsay as the athlete.

Thank you Greg, not only for not interfering, but also for guiding me by not uttering a word. In not saying a word, you said a lot. Lindsay, you too have taught me with your efforts. You, too, have taught me a lot. I love you guys.

Chapter 32

▲

CLIMBING FOR OTHERS
JAKE BOYER

"Help others achieve their dream and you will achieve yours."
    -Les Brown

198 pound Jake Boyer squatting 705 pounds at the Senior National Powerlifting
Championships.

As a college student, I had heard of Keith "Jake" Boyer because of his
competitive powerlifter exploits. Eastern Pennsylvania had a lot of great
powerlifters at the time, but none better than Jake. I knew him to be a junior-
high physical education teacher in the small town of Lehighton, Pennsylvania.
He opened a gym in Lehighton and I heard he did heavy squats on Monday
nights. A small group of us interested in powerlifting decided to drive the forty-

five minutes to see a man who weighed only 198 pounds squat 650 pounds. We hoped to pick his brain and see if he could make us stronger as well. We called and made plans to meet him on a Monday night and watch his heavy squat session.

When we walked into the gym, we were surprised by how many high school kids were there training. More surprising, we saw senior citizens. At that time, senior citizens rarely weight trained. We sat quiet and watched Jake and his two training partners progress through the warm-up sets from 135 pounds to 675 pounds. Back then, 675 pounds in squat was world class, a real treat for us. Lifters today squat more, but much of that has to do with the supportive suits and wraps that can add up to two hundred pounds to a person's squat. Regardless, we enjoyed seeing this lift, which he made with ease. We talked amongst ourselves, and waited for the chance to sit and chat with Jake. When his workout ended, we had the chance.

"Mr. Boyer, thank you for giving us the opportunity to watch you lift," I said. "It was a thrill for us to see you make that lift with room to spare."

"Thank you," he said. "But that really isn't that important. I hope you guys saw how many high school kids we had in here. I'm proud of that. These are kids that aren't well off monetarily and may go through life without a lot of chances at big things. I've worked hard to make this affordable for them and I try to give them quality instruction and a lot of love. By the way, did you also see our pumping grannies? That's why I'm here. If we can get these ladies out of the house and keep them fit, they'll be much better off than their friends and classmates that who are sitting around in nursing homes deteriorating."

He surprised us with this speech. The man we just watched squat 675 pounds thought of others first. It left us speechless. We didn't learn any powerlifting secrets that night, but we left with the sense we had learned something more important.

A few years later, I had to fulfill an undergraduate teaching requirement before graduating from East Stroudsburg State College (now East Stroudsburg University). I knew where I wanted to do my assignment, Lehighton Junior High School. I called Jake Boyer and asked him if he would be willing to take on a student teacher. I figured this would give me the chance to learn more about powerlifting and life from him. He agreed.

1980 photo of Jake coaching in the gym he set up for the betterment of the community.

To my surprise, I didn't learn as much about powerlifting during my three months at Lehighton Junior High School as I wish I had. I learned about giving to others, the lesson Jake Boyer hoped to teach me. I learned that he had started as a physical education teacher because he believed in the inherent benefits of exercise and wanted to share this with kids. He opened his gym to offer more, though he put himself at financial risk by purchasing equipment with the savings of his small teaching salary. He loved his gym and what he could do for others. This led him to the next step, purchasing a huge vacated factory. He turned the old factory into a gym single-handedly.   For three years, he worked in the factory before he started his teaching day. Then, after getting out of work, went back to the factory for another five hours. For those three years he slept in the building, obsessed. His rationale was he figured that if he could help a small number of people in a small gym, he could help ten times that number of people in a gym ten times the size. He sanded every inch of the wood floors, replaced the fifty-year-old toilets, and painted every inch of the monstrous old factory.

Jake then went back to school to earn his doctoral degree. He later told me that an administrator could impact more students than a teacher. He became an administrator, then a principal, then the superintendent of an entire district. Jake Boyer did not do any of these things for Jake Boyer. He went through years of living in an abandoned factory and laboring over its renovations. He put twelve hours a day into his full-time job. Put tens of thousands of dollars into higher education and endured the stress and time needed to acquire administrative certificates and his doctoral degree—for others. Somehow in the midst of this, he managed to squat 705 pounds in the Senior National Powerlifting Championships, a meet he placed second in.

Jake believed that the higher he could climb, the more he could impact others, and so he climbed relentlessly. In fact, he impacted and changed many, many lives. May we all live by his philosophy.

Chapter 33

SHARING BEAUTY
JESSI COLTER

"In every man's heart there is a secret nerve that answers to the vibrations of beauty."
  -Christopher Morley

Photo by Charles Gaurean

Jessi Colter and I are from different planets. Jessi comes from the world of music, a fine art. I have no musical ability. I'm from the world of martial arts. Jessi is sweet. I am focused. Jessi is quiet. I am boisterous. Jessi is pretty. My face bears the scars and crooked nose of too many martial arts. Jessi has toured the world and entertained packed houses. I prefer to be in an empty dojo, or fighting with just a few training partners. Jessi had a high profile marriage to the late, great country singer, Waylon Jennings. In contrast, my idea of happiness involves quiet evenings home with my wife Janet. Jessi has produced top-ranked country music hits worldwide. I've been hit by people worldwide. In many ways, we could not be further apart.

When I first started training Jessi seven years ago, we both underwent an interesting observation process. I had no understanding of the genius it takes to become a world-renowned musician for four decades. I knew nothing of the complications of that lifestyle. Nor did I know that musicians could have the sort of depth that Jessi has. Likewise, she had no understanding of me, my strict

training and eating regimen, or my disdain for the pleasures that consume people—junk food, fast food, and alcohol—which hold no interest for me. We didn't understand each other when we met, not at all. For that reason, we studied each other with intensity.

The beautiful Jessi Colter with my mother Jessica having fun at a party on the roof of Jessi's house.

Despite being polar opposites, I've grown to adore Jessi Colter, as a friend. She is one of those beautiful women who started off as a beautiful girl and remained that way, decades later. The combination of her angelic voice and passion for music is responsible for her many hits. Philosophical in nature, she has always been there for me, sharing her innermost thoughts. We talk about her life with Waylon Jennings and of her mother being a preacher long before it was acceptable to society. We talk about the many places she has seen in the world, her Christian faith, her children, her puppy, and most everything else. She has kept me listening, intently, for hours at a time.

If I had to choose a word for Jessi Colter, I would not use the word musician, though. Nor would I use mother, friend, philosopher, or many of the other labels that describe her. I would use the word beautiful. She has a beautiful appearance, a beautiful smile, a beautiful voice. I'm thankful that our planets collided, and more thankful that Jessi has been so willing to share her beauty. Since we are so different, I would have missed out getting to know her if she hadn't taken the time to share her beauty liberally. As per her philosophical lead, I like to imagine how much better this world would be if everyone liberally shared their particular beauty with others.

Chapter 34

TO BE PROACTIVE AND SELF-RELIANT
JOE CAJIC

"To be idle is a short road to death and to be diligent is a way of life; foolish people are idle, wise people are diligent."
-Buddha

Some time in the early 1990s, while I was serving as the Arizona State University (ASU) strength and conditioning coach, the telephone rang in the weight room. It was the football office asking me to come up and meet a new member of the team, Joe Cajic, who had just transferred from the University of Southern California (USC). A few years earlier, it had been a huge recruiting coup for USC to steal the Phoenix native away from ASU. But Joe hadn't liked USC and so he came back home to play in front of his family and friends.

At that time, I had a great graduate assistant, Evan Marcus, who has since gone on to have a career as a strength and conditioning coach for both collegiate and professional teams, most recently the Miami Dolphins. I was exceptionally busy, and due to severe understaffing, was working eighty hours per week. Evan was ready to handle more responsibility, and so I asked him to consult with Joe and to draw up an individualized exercise prescription to help Joe optimize his performance. They met, and Evan asked all of the right questions.

An hour later, Evan showed up in my office asking if he could sit down and talk. "Coach Mac, I need your help. We have a serious problem here and I'm not sure what to do."

"What's the problem, Evan? I think you can handle anything in this field."

"He has two bad shoulders, a bad knee and a bad neck. For God's sake, I can't even put him on the neck machine. I don't know what he can do," Evan said. I roared with laughter. I had never encountered anything like it. I had put Evan—who was both competent and diligent—in a no-win situation. Cajic hadn't chosen ASU to begin with. He didn't like USC, and didn't make things work there. Now that he was all jazzed up about coming back to a place he didn't like the first time around, he couldn't actually do anything. This is the type of thing you let your graduate assistant coaches handle, and I did.

Days turned into weeks and weeks turned into months. Evan worked with Joe, and did a wonderful job of helping him. Joe worked like a dog and never missed a session. I found myself growing fond of Joe. Months turned into years and Joe, now calling himself "Chych," (the Croatian pronunciation of his last name) became one of my favorite people. Chych was more than the typical meathead offensive lineman. He loved football, and we trained seven days a week to bring out his potential. He lifted weights and ran with the team. On off days, we went to boxing gyms and ran mountains. He even spent a considerable amount of time practicing Greco-Roman wrestling with Olympic silver medalist, Matt Ghaffari. We left no stone unturned in his development, but Joe was more than just a football player. Quick with a smile, he was a great student, who loved to study world culture and Russian literature, and was genuinely a pleasure to be around. Lord knows, I spent enough time with this guy—three to four hours a day, six days a week.

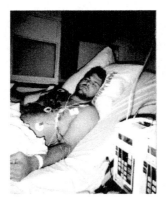

A few years after his college career ended, I heard the startling news that Chych had leukemia. This type of leukemia could not be treated with chemotherapy and he was told that one of two things had to happen. He would either find a bone marrow transplant donor or he would die within three years. The chances of him finding the perfect match to his bone marrow needs were slim. In fact, they were one in a million.

"It's the hardest thing in the world to tell your parents you might die. I just remember the look on my dad's face," Joe said.

Joe attended counseling; when your chances are one in a million, it's tough to remain positive. He told his counselors that because he was of Croatian descent, he knew it would be even more difficult to find a donor. He wanted to facilitate the process by whatever means possible. His counselor told him, emphatically, that he should not seek to rectify the problem himself. The stress would only contribute to his body's rapid deterioration.

Though Joe heard the words and understood them, he disregarded the recommendation. He attended a Croatian-American conference, along with nine thousand others. He convinced the founders to let him make an announcement.

"My name is Joe Cajic. I am an American of Croatian descent. My parents came to America from Croatia. I am dying of leukemia and have two and a half years to live, at best. I need to have a bone marrow transplant and my chances of finding success are one in a million in the typical American society. I believe my chances would be higher in a Croatian population, and ask that if any of you are willing to be tested to please come see me in the hallway. The cost of the test is about $50.00. Thank you."

Joe went out into the hallway and waited. No one showed up. Finally a man approached him and asked him how many people had volunteered.

"No one has shown up, sir," Joe said. "All I can think of is that people don't want to pay money to get jabbed with a needle."

That man wrote Joe a check on the spot for $9,000. Joe went back to the microphone and announced that anyone willing to be tested, thanks to the donation of a wonderful anonymous man, could do so for free. He had hundreds line up.

Joe not only searched for the marrow that would save his own life, but he formed the "Save Joe Foundation." His non-profit organization raised funds to provide free bone marrow testing and educate the public about leukemia,

Hodgkin's disease, and other cancers that require bone marrow transplants.

It seemed certain Joe would die, but if he was going to die, he was going to save others. So he worked around the clock. With the help of NHL hockey player Joe Sakic (of Croatian descent), and Al Molina, president of Molina Fine Jewelers, the Save Joe Foundation hosted fund raising events, including a black tie boxing event. Dozens of people found their bone marrow matches through Joe's program. Joe wasn't one of them.

Some two years later, Joe, the former stud offensive lineman at Arizona State University, received "the call." A match had been found, though not by his program. They cautioned him not to get too excited, because even though they found a match, the procedure doesn't work most of the time. The match they'd found was a graduate of the University of Arizona, the arch rival of the school Joe played for. Wildcats saving lives of Sun Devils; there's something you don't think about every day when you're a huge fan of one or the other.

Months after the bone marrow transplant, his friends and family got the first of a series of E-mails that we would continue receiving for the next two

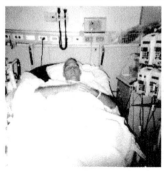

years. They each said something to the effect of, "If you have anything you need to say to Joe, this is probably the right time, because things don't look good for him." Look good, they didn't. Over those next few years Joe went through the bone marrow transplant and radiation, had a hole punched in his heart, and underwent numerous other risky procedures. He should have died many times, but always seemed to hang on.

One of many days good ole Joe fought his battle.

When Joe finally left the hospital he came to me to start an exercise program. He was allowed to walk on the treadmill for five minutes, and boy was he excited. He showed up virtually unrecognizable. His face had nearly doubled its original size, which is quite a feat since the players at ASU called

Even though the prednisone caused a moon face comparable to a basketball or head of cabbage, Joe and his father never lost their sense of humor.

him Fred Flintstone—even before the treatments—because of his big head. Joe took ninety milligrams of prednisone every day for months at a time. He had no hair. He looked like some sort of James Bond villain, but he was thrilled to walk his five minutes.

Five minutes is about the amount of time it took us to get him on the treadmill. It wasn't pretty. He simply could not step up the eight inches to get on it, even with much assistance. Undaunted, he finally made it, but had to rest after struggling like that, and had to wait a little longer before he could start his actual five minutes of walking. I think the process of getting him on the treadmill, resting, walking, resting again, and getting him off the treadmill took him over a half an hour. But Joe was determined, and so were we. It wasn't until months later that he confessed he'd been told he could walk two to three minutes, and not five.

Despite the leukemia, prednisone, hole in his heart, and frequent near-death experiences, Joe put in every hour he could to help save others. He was good at it, too. He even talked me into donating the watch and ring I had received as an Assistant Strength Coach for the 1987 Rose Bowl team. Joe's foundation raised some $3900 from the ring and watch alone.

Joe Cajic is alive today, and against all odds, is doing well. He works; he's happy; he dates; and he is still that same happy-go-lucky, wonderful friend. Not to dismiss the contributions of those who council the terminally ill, but Joe changed his life, the day he chose to be pro-active and self-reliant. He gave himself something to live for, and while doing so, saved hundreds of others and served as a most brilliant of teachers.

▲

Chapter 35

PROFESSIONAL TEAMWORK
ROB ALBERINO AND RICH GENTILE

"Teamwork is the ability to work together toward a common vision. The ability to direct individual accomplishment toward organization objectives. It is the fuel that allows common people to attain uncommon results."
-Unknown

Throughout my three decades of employment in various places, I have had many amazing, life-altering experiences. I've met people I've greatly admired, people who taught me much, and people who have become lifelong friends. Many of those I have written about in this book came into my life because of my employment.

This isn't to say that I look through rose-colored glasses or that I imagine the daily grind to be a little slice of heaven. In fact, most of the environments I have worked in left me wondering why the supposed leadership didn't place more emphasis on cohesiveness or good ole' team effort. After decades of this, I settled on the notion that this is just the way it is; work environments will always operate this way given egos, politics, and the what's-in-it-for-me syndrome.

I'm pretty sure this is why Rob Alberino and Rich Gentile entered into my life. These guys are the perfect example of how one plus one can equal far more than two.

Rob and Rich produced shows for the Philadelphia Eagles Television Network. I met them in 2000, when they came out to film Warren Anderson and me training Donovan McNabb and Charles Johnson. Ultra-professional and courteous, they never got in the way of drills, and they even volunteered when needed. In that way, they exceeded any expectations I had, having dealt with media for twenty years. That wasn't the impressive part, though. They impressed me most with their teamwork.

Rob and Rich both served as leader and follower in their filming and photography. When Rob led a task, Rich stepped in as an assistant, playing the role to perfection. Rich seemed to anticipate Rob's needs. Then the task would change and Rich would emerge as the alpha and Rob would follow Rich's lead, as if he had been Rich's assistant for life.

After a day of this, I was awed. That sort of cohesiveness just doesn't happen in the work environment. And yet, they came back the next year, and nothing had changed. In 110 degree heat, Rich ran agility drills with the running athletes while holding a camera, but Rob was there every step of the way to ensure good quality. Year three, exactly the same. Year four, five, and six, exactly the same. They seemed to have fun and function like two hands on the same body. I am embarrassed to admit that because they worked so closely together, I sometimes called them by each other's names.

Rob and Rich are talented young go-getters. I've seen their work on television broadcasts and the big screens at Franklin Field. I am grateful to have learned from them what the work environment can and should be. Better yet, I am grateful to have seen it year after year. For years, I wondered why, in many of the environments I worked in, the leaders left their departments divided and functioning at less than their capacity. After seeing these great individuals working as a team I know what sort of productivity is possible. Thank you Rob and Rich; you have produced so much more in my life than just the television shows you were working on.

135

Chapter 36

CHOOSING A GOOD ATTITUDE
TODD VAN BODEGOM-SMITH

"When life gives you lemons, make lemonade."
  -Unknown

We have all heard stories about the guys who "never catch a break" or "get all the bad luck." I am not one of those guys, but I have met one. His name is Todd Van Bodegom-Smith.

I met Todd in 1979, when a few of us undergraduate physical education majors decided to form a powerlifting team at East Stroudsburg State College. To assess interest, we placed an ad in the *Stroud Courier*, our school newspaper. The ad requested that anyone who wanted to lift should call my dorm room, and Todd called first. I've never told Todd this story, but I thought his

phone call was a prank. He was too outgoing, too pumped up, too friendly. And then, real people just don't have names like Van Bodegom-Smith. Even with his simple, enthusiastic inquiry, Todd couldn't catch a break.

After checking with the hall director and finding that one Todd Van Bodegom-Smith indeed existed, I went to meet him. Todd had powerlifting experience. He had competed in the Garden State Teenage Championship, in the 148 pound class. He told me during our talk that he wanted to be a 148 pounder. Why did it have to be the 148 pound class? I wondered. We had one phenomenally strong person on the team at that time, Mark Shelhamer. Mark was, of course, a 148 pounder. Todd just couldn't catch a break.

The team grew over the next few years and several of the lifters became national class. Todd took seven years to graduate. After graduation he revealed to me that he was severely dyslexic, and something that I could read in an hour would take him four hours to read and his retention rate would be lower.

We all loved the Todd stories we heard over the years, like the time he missed the five o'clock deadline for turning in an end-of-term paper. The paper represented fifty percent of his grade. The professor said he would accept papers until five on Friday. If papers hadn't been turned in at that time, it was automatic failure for the semester. Todd, of course, showed up at 4:45 pm only to find that the professor had left, and there was no way to get the paper to him.

What's a man to do in this circumstance? Todd didn't want to fail the course and have to repeat it. Later that night, he and an unnamed accomplice dressed from head to toe in black ninja-like gear, scaled the walls, and broke into the building. He had no intention of changing a grade or stealing a test, merely of turning in a paper he had been promised he could turn in by 5:00 p.m. on Friday. He planned to find the stack of papers, insert his own, and leave.

Todd made himself as stealthy as the best of ninjas and scaled the wall like a spelunking champion. He jimmied the window open and climbed through. Todd was catching a break...until he found he had climbed into the wrong office.

He was in office number 209 and not 210. Some guys just can't catch a break.

Shortly after graduation, Todd became very ill. This caught all of us by surprise, since Todd was the one guy in the group who was far more full of life than any of the rest of us. He was diagnosed with a life-threatening case of Lyme disease. The illness went on for years and contributed to a divorce that would affect him deeply. Later, he was told he didn't have Lyme disease, but no one could figure what made him so sick.

Several more years passed before Todd had an answer. It seemed like a big break for Todd when his doctor told him he'd finally figured out what made him sick, except that it turned out to be amyotrophic lateral sclerosis—in slang terms, ALS or Lou Gehrig's disease. ALS took the life of baseball great Lou Gehrig—the man with the best natural swing in the history of the game—

After many episodes of Todd trying to psych himself up by banging his head on the bar until he bled, we finally decided to document the event.

and the lives of just about everyone else it ever affected. There is no cure. This once mighty powerlifter, who would bang his head on a bar until it bled to psych himself up, now has arms literally a third the size they had been in his lifting prime.

This isn't to say that Todd's whole life has been a downer. It hasn't. Indeed, Todd could never catch a break. But still, this chapter is about how extraordinary Todd, my friend, teacher, and teammate, truly is.

Despite the unfair number of hardships Todd endured, from dyslexia to a life ending illness, Todd never let it get him down. I don't know how he does it; I just marvel. Todd is vivacious, fun, funny, and giving. Todd can relate to anyone, no matter how aloof, young, arrogant, or unfriendly. Time spent with Todd seems like time spent with a comedian, while performing.

I have wondered for well over a decade how any guy could ever have such great character, let alone a guy who could never catch a break. This includes the time he was in Jim Cope's car, riding back to campus and he jokingly told Jim that he thought Jim would never become a national class powerlifter. Jim, true to his fired up ways back then, kicked Todd out of his car and made him walk four miles back to their off-campus apartment. As Todd later recanted, "the first mile wasn't bad: it's when the freezing rain and hail started that it got truly uncomfortable." Only Todd...

Thank you Todd Van Bodegom-Smith, a man with a funny personality and a funny last name. You were the perfect messenger in my life to teach me that a man can have a lot of lousy things happen in his life without having a lousy day. You are my hero.

Chapter 37

EXTREME COMPETENCE
ANGELO PARISI

"It was accepted in feudal Japan that when two samurai met on a battlefield, that one had to die. It is important to train in this spirit, to try and acquire this skill."
  -Judo Sensei Riki Adamcik

I think many people recognize Miyamoto Musashi as the greatest martial artist who ever lived. As an accomplished swordsman with an unbeatable reputation in ancient Japan, he was challenged throughout his career by every top swordsman in the land. In total, he was challenged and fought to the death 60 times. His record, of course, was 60 to 0. This sort of domination by a warrior is unparalleled in history. I think of Miyamoto Musashi when I hear the name Angelo Parisi. I have this association because of the unusually dominant performance he laid on us one night at Sensei Christophe Leininger's dojo. I will never forget that night.

Class started at 6:30 p.m., as usual. And as on all other nights, the dojo was packed with young, fit, strong judo black belts. After all, Leininger's dojo was the place to be for fighters. I could often find twenty or more national class black belts—the sort who lived to fight—on any given night. Christophe himself was a national champion multiple times. His brother Brian was another national champion. Jim Dunning, Eric Udell, Werner Van Hayes, Doug Hyde, Walter VanHelder, David Brinn, Tony Erickson, Kurt Bebe, Oscar Fuchsbaum— the list of thoroughly lethal men goes on. The Japanese have a term, "jigoku kego." Roughly translated, it means "hell training." Our three times a week workout at Leininger's, two and a half hours at a time, qualifies as jigoku kego. No one died, but we all came close several times a week.

We had two guest instructors that particular night, Jacques Noris and Angelo Parisi, from France. Because I knew how good French judo was, I thought this might be a night with more technical instruction. The first half of class went as I predicted. Jacques did all of the teaching while Angelo said virtually nothing, remaining a complete mystery to us.

Once fighting starts, no one stands around to watch at the Leininger dojo. If twenty are present, they divide into ten groups of two. At the end of the designated fight time (usually five minutes), partners switch within ten seconds and the next fight begins. One five minute fight with a national class competitor is brutal; doing it eight to ten times, consecutively, is horrible.

Three quarters of the way through our matches, I was paired up with Angelo. What a massive, quiet guy, I thought. His ankles looked like tree trunks. His wrists looked like tree trunks. The rest of him looked like the Rock of Gibraltar. He was obviously physically imposing, but he was also quiet. Since I knew nothing about him, I wondered if he would fight well. I was about to find out.

Sensei Christophe yelled "hajime" and we started to fight. I grabbed onto Angelo's gi top and tried de ashi barai, a foot sweep used to knock his foot out from under him. I whacked that big sucker hard, but he didn't move—like whacking a tree trunk. At this point, he made eye contact with me and lifted up his left foot off the mat, as if to say, "You wanted my foot off the ground, so I'll fight you with my foot off of the ground." Since I've often been called "more enthusiasm than intellect," I immediately tried to sweep the only foot he had on the ground. This time I whacked that big sucker twice as hard. He nodded slightly. As I wondered what that subtle nod meant, I started my flight. That big sucker that I tried to foot sweep twice flung me over his head at the speed of light, like a human cannon ball. This is called ippon, and would make him an instant winner in a judo match. But this was training and not a match, so it did not end. And since I am more enthusiasm than intellect, I got up and went after him again. This cycle repeated itself eight times in those five minutes. Eight times I achieved the same outcome. I tried to throw him and he turned me into a human projectile. There is nothing on earth I could have done that night to beat that man or even score on him.

I saw, felt, and understood how judo could be taken to extreme competency that night. After he'd thrown me for the eighth time—and I'd gone airborne for the eighth time—Sensei Christophe yelled, "Thirty seconds left." I looked up at Angelo and muttered without realizing I had done so.

This mountain of a man looked at me and said, in a thick French accent, "What's wrong?"

"There are only thirty seconds left and the score is about forty-eight to zero." I said. He laughed.

After the fighting and class ended, I got a recovery drink and sat down with my wife Janet. "That was really embarrassing," I said. "I can't believe I got dominated that way."

She said about the only thing that could have made me feel better at the time. "He did the same thing to Christophe. He chucked him all over the place."

"Really?" I asked.

"Absolutely," Janet said. "If he threw the best person in this country in your weight class like a rag doll, how would you expect to do better?"

After class I introduced myself to Angelo in the locker room. There I learned he was the Olympic gold medalist in the heavyweight division, a higher weight class than my own. He was kind enough to sign an autograph for me that reads, "To Tim: Best wishes for your judo. Angelo Parisi, 50–0." Apparently the man has a world-class sense of humor as well.

Regardless, he taught me what extreme competence in judo looks like. What I saw from him has made me strive for better performance in all areas of my life. Thank you, Angelo. I now know who you are, and will never forget.

Chapter 38

▲

TRUSTWORTHINESS
JEFF DECKER

"I judge a person's worth by the kind of person he is in life – by the way he treats his fellow man, by the way he wants to be treated, and by the way he respects people around him."
-Calvin Murphy

There isn't much I wouldn't do to help Jeff Decker. I know there isn't much he wouldn't do to help me. This is the way our friendship works, and has worked for twenty years.

Twenty years ago, Jeff Decker walked on to play football at Arizona State University. I was their strength and conditioning coach, in charge of all aspects of training for the football program, which, naturally, included preparing Jeff.

Walk-ons can be difficult to help; most do not have the playing skills they need to succeed at that level—which is why they were not offered scholarships in the first place. Often they seem to think their skills are better than they truly are, which causes a whole new set of problems: they don't have the skill to play, but are upset when they don't get playing time. Jeff was never one of those guys. He kept quiet and showed how badly he wanted to play with the tremendous effort he put in. Unlike most others, Jeff actually had the skills to play major college football.

The more my staff and I got to work with Jeff, the more we grew to trust and respect him. The more work we gave him and the more we pushed him, the harder he worked. In turn, the harder he worked, the more we respected him, so we gave him even more work. Back then, in my young and crazy coaching days, I wasn't afraid of training anyone into the ground. Jeff Decker got that training program six times a week. I knew that for him to make the team and make it on the field, we had to put him through some extraordinary measures. Unlike most walk-ons, Jeff went through those crazy workouts every day, without complaint, and contributed significantly as a senior at ASU. Once, he was on the kick-off team and had the job of running full speed to take out a blocker in the opposing team's wedge. Jeff was not the fastest guy on the kick-off team, but as usual, he was the first man down the field on that kick-off. He torpedoed himself into three blockers, disabling three men at once. Unfortunately, this resulted in a severe concussion for Jeff. But that didn't dampen his enthusiasm or effort.

More than a decade has passed since I crushed him in the weight room, or since that concussion, which left him lying lifeless on the turf at Sun Devil Stadium for what seemed like an eternity. Since then, we have practiced martial arts together and fought like two bobcats. We've been mean and we've been ruthless. At times, I've gone out to help him coach high school kids for hours at a time in the scorching heat of Phoenix, and at times he has helped me move around entire weight rooms. Six hours of carrying weights and weight machines is about the worst sort of work out there, and yet he's helped me through all of it.

We've had some challenging times, but two things have been constant. The first is that I know I can always trust and count on Jeff Decker. Regardless of the task, or how much it will hurt, or what else he has to accomplish in life, I know Jeff Decker will be there for me. The second is that I always want to be there to reciprocate. I would be honored to think that someday, somebody somewhere will see me as a man as trustworthy as I see Jeff Decker.

Chapter 39

BELIEVING IN YOURSELF
DENNIS HAYDEN

"Never let the odds keep you from doing what you know in your heart you were meant to do."

    -H. Jackson Brown Jr.

In 1985, I was elevated from graduate-assistant strength and conditioning coach to full-time assistant strength and conditioning coach at Arizona State University. As such, I assisted in all phases of strength and conditioning for the football team and ran training programs for the other twenty-five sports. To begin, I arranged meetings with the head coach of each team to tell them what we offered and to figure out how to best help their athletes.

I met with Don Robinson first, the men's gymnastics coach. I'd heard Don was a progressive coach, very positive, and possibly the nicest guy on the staff. A good place to start, I thought. Memorabilia covered every inch of his office walls—cups from team championships, plaques, trophies, miscellaneous gifts from coaches all over the world (whose teams Don Robinson's team had beaten.) I was supposed to tell this man how I could make his team better, and yet, in front of me hung twenty-five years worth of proof that his teams did quite well all on their own. Still, I knew the NCAA takes the top four teams in the country to compete in the team championship finals, and that his team had missed that final the year before by five hundredths of a point. I thought I could help make at least that bit of difference.

As we talked, I turned my head to the right and what I saw made me jump off the chair. Until then I hadn't noticed the kangaroo head mounted on the wall alongside me, apparently a gift from an Australian coach. When I made eye contact with the kangaroo I thought it was a living animal. That broke the ice, and became a story we would talk about for twenty years. In the meantime, we decided that if I could help make a difference of one-tenth of a point in even one performer, Don's team could possibly be a legitimate contender for the NCAA championship.

Don agreed to give it a try, and he told me he had a special project, to rehabilitate Dennis Hayden. Dennis had torn his anterior cruciate ligament (ACL) while dismounting a high bar at the 1985 NCAA championships in Nebraska. Dennis had a twin brother, Dan, and together they ranked as two of the top gymnasts in the entire United States, not just among collegians. Both planned to compete for Don that season, although Dennis was doing so against medical advice and without having his torn ACL surgically repaired.

I took to the team instantly, not just the Hayden brothers—who were two of the greatest kids anyone could ever coach—but also Jerry Burrell, Mike Zarillo, Mark Bowers, John Sweeney, Mike Wolf and the rest of the team. After all, this was Don Robinson's team, and Don Robinson's team is not a team—it's a family.

The team worked hard. Workouts scheduled for an hour invariably lasted two. They held weighted pull-up contests, weighted dip contests, and somehow even talked my assistant Rich Wenner and me into a handstand contest on the metal racks used to hold free weights.

I spent a great deal of time carefully constructing Dennis Hayden's programs, to provide his legs with the strength and stability they would need to compete without his ACL. This seemed like a long shot to me, because everyone I consulted—from orthopedic surgeons to athletic trainers to athletes with torn ACLs—said it couldn't be done. Only one person felt it could be done: Dennis Hayden.

Sensei Andy Bauman taught me about his Ja Shin Do martial art style, which literally means, path of self belief. But really, I learned even more from Dennis Hayden about that path. I do not know why the number three ranked gymnast in the entire United States would elect to not have surgery, but he always assured me that with proper work and a caring, and a patient coach, he could pull it off. He knew in his heart he could make it work.

To make a long story short, the following year, ASU made it to the final four and earned a right to compete for the National Championship. I was thrilled. I had hoped this family I had coached would be successful, and that I had made some slight difference in everyone's performance. But if I had helped just one person, all of my efforts would have been worth it.

During team finals, the other three teams had just finished their final rotation, and Arizona State remained as the last team on the floor competing. In fact, only two Arizona State competitors were left, the flying Hayden brothers. Their last event was the high bar, the same high bar in the same gym where Dennis Hayden tore his ACL a year earlier. The scores were tallied. To win, Arizona State needed Dennis Hayden to score a whopping 9.8 (a very high score for a collegian) and his twin, Dan, would need a 9.9. Why did it have to be that very same high bar? Thousands of high bars exist in this county, and yet Dennis Hayden had to compete and score a 9.8 on that very same high bar, without the surgery everyone in the world told him he needed. This seemed like asking someone to pull an elephant out of a hat, forget the rabbit.

Dennis Hayden scored a 9.8 that day. I am still not sure how. It must have had something to do with his extraordinary self-belief. A quiet, polite, and very humble kid, Dennis Hayden just knew he could do it. Dennis's brother Dan, competing to win or lose the team's national championship, was the focal point in the gym as he scored his 9.95.

I learned a lot from these kids I coached. I learned a lot from Don Robinson.

He saturated his gymnasts with discipline and desire, as well as love, positive thinking, and self belief. Dennis Hayden was the role model for that.

In my humble opinion, Dennis Hayden, Dan Hayden, Don Robinson and the rest of the team all get perfect 10's.

Chapter 40

PARENTAL LOVE
KEN

"There is no friendship, no love, like that of the parent for the child."
  -Henry Ward Beecher

I work with many hopeful athletes between the ages of twelve and twenty. By working with great kids, I have been fortunate enough to also meet many amazing parents. This chapter is dedicated to a particularly wonderful parent, my late father, Ken McClellan. I wish I could read this to him on the back porch of my childhood country home, but I suppose I'll have to wait until I see him in heaven.

My father couldn't beat up your father, but my father came to all of my Little League games. He also came to all of my football games. As if that weren't enough, he attended every basketball game I ever played. He was not the prototypical "soccer mom," obsessive with helping his son become the next professional star. He was a man who gave parental love. He gave support, encouragement, and a huge piece of his heart.

I can't imagine how bored he must have been at times, watching fifth grade boys try to play tackle football. Scores in those games often ended 6 to 0. He watched these same kids play thirty or more games of baseball a year, and another twenty games of basketball, in which games often ended with a combined score of forty points or less. He never missed a game and he never complained about how bad the play was at times. When we won, his smile was so big it seemed as though he had won. I will never forget that special feeling we shared after victories.

I played quite a few bad games in all sports. Everyone does throughout their career. There were missed ground balls, strike outs, dropped passes, and missed lay-ups. My father encouraged me to stay with the game and learn life lessons from sports. Fortunately, there were also the touchdowns, championships, no-hitters, and three-point shots. Wow, did my dad make me feel special on those occasions. Had he not encouraged me to stick with sports through the missed ground balls and lay-ups, I would never have been able to enjoy those accomplishments.

In my senior year of high school, I was selected co-captain of the football team. My father worked for a company that required him to travel to the other end of the state for business. He audited radio stations and was required to be on-site for Friday evenings, but he never was. Every Friday, he found someone in a western Pennsylvania town to tape-record the radio programs he was supposed to be taping, and he paid that person cash out of his own pocket to do the work. He then drove six hours just to watch me and our team play our football games. Every Saturday, on only four or five hours of sleep, he would kiss my mother goodbye and drive back another six hours. He would leave me with the game program from the night before, and it was always mangled, crumbled up from his nervousness when either the team or I struggled. Twelve hours of driving and four hours of sleep every week to support a son. That is special parenting. He never pushed me to be a superstar or scholarship winner. He just gave me all he had to support my dream. His passing in 1986, due to complications from diabetes, left a definitive void in my life. I had always wanted him to see me become a head Strength and Conditioning Coach at a major university. I did not achieve that until 1987. This life experience has made me sensitive to this day of the need to help those brought up in a single parent family.

When it's all said and done, there are families with nicer cars and more money, but I ended up rich because of the mentoring, love, support and guidance my father gave me when I needed it most. Thank you, Dad. I know you'll have a warm greeting for me when we reunite in heaven.

Proud father Kenneth at my college graduation, aside grandmothers "Mac" (left) and "Nan" (far right), and mother Jessica (second from left).

Chapter 41

THE POWER OF DREAMS
KENDALL CROSS

"Have great hopes and dare to go all out for them. Have great dreams and dare to live them. Have tremendous expectations and believe in them."
-Norman Vincent Peale

The amazing Kendall Cross on the podium after winning the 1996 Olympic Games in freestyle wrestling.

When I met Kendall Cross in 1995, I never would have envisioned the amazing story that was about to unfold.

Kendall was a successful collegiate wrestler at Oklahoma State University. After he graduated, he made the 1992 USA Olympic Wrestling team. At the time, a medal was not really a consideration. Kendall was simply not good enough to be amongst the top three when competing against the world's best. His best hope to medal was the 1996 Olympics. He would need four years of intense training to do so. As Kendall found out, a huge obstacle would stand in the way of his even making the 1996 team: a beast named Terry Brands.

In 1993, Kendall was beaten on his own turf by Brands. As in the Olympics, only one wrestler from each country can compete in the World Championship. And so in 1993, it was Brands - not Kendall - who went. Brands was a Collegiate National Champion at the University of Iowa and was under the guidance of wrestling legend, Dan Gable. Anyone who wrestled for Gable was an animal on the mat. Under Gable's coaching, the Iowa team won ten consecutive NCAA championships. Iowa wrestlers had a reputation for being cock-strong, fit, and tougher than nails. Brands epitomized this.

In 1993, Brands went on to win the World Championship. In 1994 he beat Kendall for the right to compete in the World Championships again. In 1995, the pre-Olympic year, Brands won the World Championship for the second time. He was surely the best in the world.

Things didn't look good for Kendall, but Kendall had a dream. In fact, he lived by a quote that year: "Happy are those that dream dreams and enthusiastically pay the price to make them come true."

After a full year of training to beat Brands—which involved watching videotapes of Brands just about every day—Kendall beat him for the right to go to the 1996 Olympic Games in Atlanta. This somewhat distressed the wrestling community in the USA. Kendall had done his homework to beat Brands, but hadn't wrestled in the World Championships the previous three years, and hadn't done all that well against international competition in the previous Olympics. Brands had defeated all of the top foreigners; he'd shown the world he had the composure, skill, and technical capability to win gold. Most thought Terry Brands would have done better than Kendall. The prognosticators hadn't factored in the power of Kendall's dreams.

I first met Kendall at the pre-Olympic training camp in Colorado Springs. I was the strength and conditioning coach for the USA Wrestling team. I'd worked with several team members the year before. The guys I'd coached in the past were glad to have their normal conditioning coach with them, and the guys I hadn't worked with were receptive to my help. Then we moved to a second camp, in Chattanooga, Tennessee. The USA team and alternates trained in Chattanooga for two weeks, as it was close to Atlanta. The commute from there to the games would be easy.

153

The wrestlers were housed in vacated dorms at the University of Tennessee-Chattanooga. They wrestled on mats on the basketball court and had access to both a weight room overlooking the basketball courts and a training table for meals. Airdyne bicycles were set out nightly in the quadrant adjoining the dorms so those who needed to make weight could burn extra calories. Kendall Cross was one of those wrestlers.

One evening, I went door to door to discuss the strength training, flexibility, and massage needs of the team members for the following day. In addition to me—their strength and conditioning coach—USA Wrestling had hired Marie Finamore, a massage therapist on her third Olympic tour with USA Wrestling, and Ann Frederick, a stretch guru with skills second to none.

This particular evening, I banged on Kendall's door. I knew he was overweight and I was concerned about his welfare. Upon hearing the knock, he yelled for me to enter. I did so and immediately burst out laughing. Kendall had apparently wanted to watch television while he cut weight; he was pedaling an Airdyne bike he'd stolen from the quadrant, while he wore a plastic sweat suit.

"Hi Kendall. I'm just stopping by to see how you are, and to see if there's anything you need. How much are you over?"

"Twenty-seven," he said.

"How long are you riding, Kendall?"

"Four," he replied.

I must be confusing numbers, I thought. Perhaps this guy is four pounds over and riding the bike for twenty-seven minutes. He surely couldn't be twenty-seven pounds overweight and starting a ride of four hours, not after two practices and a conditioning session.

I was dumbfounded. This guy didn't have twenty-seven pounds of fat on him. Kendall Cross looked like he didn't have seven pounds of fat on him. There were ten days left before he wrestled in the Olympic Games. This was his last chance ever to be in the running for an Olympic medal. I just could not picture this guy losing ten pounds, let alone twenty-seven, and then being able to stand, let alone wrestle the top freestyle wrestlers in the world. In hindsight, I too underestimated the power of Kendall's dreams.

"Tim, I'm going to make it and I'm going to win," he said. "I have a dream."

Against all odds, Kendall Cross made weight. I'm quite sure every nutritionist, doctor, and exercise physiologist in this country would have said that was impossible. Kendall Cross also won the gold medal that week, against the prediction of all of the gurus of wrestling. They too had obviously underestimated the power of his dream.

In a matter of months, Kendall Cross not only beat Terry Brands, the beast who had beaten the world, but had somehow shed twenty-seven pounds off a frame that looked like it had 2.7 pounds of fat on it, and had gone on to beat the rest of the world himself. He had a dream.

Happy was he who dreamed a dream and enthusiastically paid the insurmountable price to make it come true. Happy are those with a teacher like Kendall Cross.

▲

CONTINUITY
ERIC HINSKE

"Spectacular is always preceded by spectacular achievement."
 -Dr. Robert Schuller

I met Eric Hinske when he was playing minor league baseball and hoping to transition to the major leagues. His agent at that time, Bill Moore, brought him to see me. Eric was a big, thick kid at 6'2" and 240 pounds. He was full of enthusiasm and natural athleticism. Densely muscled, he could accelerate, decelerate, and hit top speeds of a much smaller and lighter person. He had played college baseball at the University of Arkansas, and I liked that he worked hard.

I worked Eric, and several other professional baseball players, very hard that year. They were a great group of motivated guys and so the sessions were both fun and rewarding. The work-outs weren't easy, but then, the jump from minor league baseball to a permanent spot in the major leagues is never easy.

Triple-A professional baseball (minor league) players have a lot to be proud of, and players earn above-average salaries by American standards. But Eric was the sort that would probably have felt as though he failed to achieve his twenty-year dream if he hadn't made it to the major leagues. Hardworking, determined, and fun as Eric is, I cared for him and didn't want him in that position. I didn't want him to look back the rest of his life and think, of the old quote, "Of all the words known to men, the saddest are these, 'It could have been.' " Indeed, with determination and tireless effort, Eric rose from minor league ball to Major League Rookie of the Year as the Toronto Blue Jays' star third baseman within a year.

This story, however, is not about his meteoric rise from minor league ball to stardom. Rather, this story takes place throughout the years after that, during the next many seasons Eric trained with me. Eric taught me the lesson of continuity. He has returned to me season after season after season to work under my guidance. Because of his continuity, I know his physiology and psyche extraordinarily well. I can tell when he is on the verge of overtraining during our off-season work-outs. Within fifteen minutes of starting the next off-season's work-outs, I can judge his fitness level, his range of joint motion, and his functional movements as they apply to elite baseball, and how they compare to the previous season. I have a thorough, time-tested road map, so to speak, to guide him to the destination we are seeking. I have traveled this route many times, and know how to get him to his desired destination.

I have enjoyed working with Eric Hinske and being there throughout his successful transition. As in any athlete's career, he has had his highs and lows. His first season he was the American League Rookie of the Year. He also played for the World Series Champion Boston Red Sox, and the next season on what many thought would be the worst team in pro baseball, the Tampa Bay Rays. That team also played in the World Series. Broken bones in his wrist once kept him from swinging the bat correctly, causing his average to plummet. Regardless of his highs and lows, he seeks consistent guidance, something which many athletes cannot balance with the demands of a one hundred and sixty two game schedule. His continuity makes his progress easy for me to chart, and easier for me to coach him. With Eric in mind, I tell athletes, "Seek out a great coach. If you have a great coach, you need to follow his or her lead to the best of your ability, a hundred percent of the time, over a long period of time."

Doing so will enable their coach to know their physical and mental abilities better, and to serve them properly. As I write this, I think on how well our continuity has served Eric, and how his lesson of continuity will help me to be a better teacher to the athletes I coach. I also think about the next off-season, and contemplate what we will need to do to improve the program we have been molding over the past decade. I know Eric Hinske will be back next off-season and he knows I'll be ready for him. Together we will flourish, thanks to his continuity.

Chapter 43

▲

GIVING
JESSICA "THE ONE AND ONLY JESSICA"

"Others first, then yourself."
       -Anonymous

I felt honored to attend Jessica's surprise 80th birthday party. Her sister Mary lured her there with the pretense of a simple dinner, and it worked like a charm. Folks came to New Jersey from all corners of the country. Her brothers and sisters gave heartfelt testimonials, and her son Keith gave a talk that made her cry—with joy, naturally. For my own part, I was amazed by the outpour of love for Jessica.

The presents, testimonials, and demonstrations of love were heartwarming.

Brother Keith and I showing affection at Mom's 80th birthday party.

Equally interesting was Jessica's response. Appreciative beyond words, she struggled at times, because she was in an unfamiliar role. Jessica isn't usually the center of attention. Rather, for eighty years she had been the one giving the attention, giving the love, giving the presents, and doing anything within her power to benefit others. Jessica is my mother, and she has never said to me, "Others first, and then yourself." But she taught me that anyway, with her own actions.

I want to challenge everyone with a simple exercise, to put others ahead of themselves in every interaction for just one day. This means saying good morning to everyone you see before they say it to you. It means reaching out to strangers and befriending them. It means asking others if there's anything you can do to help them. It means keeping quiet about your own misfortunes and disabilities and carefully listening to others about theirs. It means taking others to lunch or dinner. As Stephen Covey, author of "The Seven Habits of Highly Effective People" says, "Seek first to understand, then to be understood." This would be a very difficult exercise for many, but imagine how happy and peaceful the world would be for just one day if everyone could make themselves do that for just those twenty-four hours out of the year.

Now imagine one person doing that for eighty years. This is the one and only Jessica, and why everyone who knows Jessica loves her.

Mom, thank you for putting my little league first, my Pop Warner football first, my college tuition, my wife, my dogs, and so forth first. In saying nothing, you said it all. You are my first teacher and your lessons are still with me. I love you.

3 years later and far up a mountain in the Arizona desert.

Chapter 44

CONTROL
MIKE BRIDGES

"The world belongs to the enthusiast who keeps his cool."
    -William McFee, "Casuals of the Sea"

1982 Senior National Powerlifting
Championships photo of the incomparable Mike Bridges.

I was hot and heavy into the powerlifting world in the late 1980s. In 1988, the American Drug Free Powerlifting Association (ADFPA) joined the newly-formed World Drug Free Powerlifting Federation. This gave competitors who preferred not to use strength enhancing drugs a fair platform. Once the association became official, the first drug-free World Championships were set to be held in Reading, England. The United States would send winners from the 1987 ADFPA national championships as the USA team. A notice was put in <u>Powerlifting USA</u> magazine that all parties interested in being considered for head coach should contact Brother Bennet, the ADFPA president. As I had coached several of the 1987 champions, I thought I had a good chance of getting the job.

When I called Brother Bennet to ask what I needed to apply, he told me off record that he had just decided, and I would be head coach. I was honored to have been selected without ever applying, and thrilled by their vote of confidence. The following year I coached the USA team in England. USA lifters won all eleven weight classes and went home happy. Thanks to the efforts and accomplishments of the lifters, I was asked to be head coach again in 1989. That year the World Championships were scheduled for Chicago.

When I arrived in Chicago for the meet, I was in for a huge thrill. I would have the honor of coaching 181 pound lifter Mike Bridges. Mike Bridges may be the greatest powerlifter in the history of the world in any weight class. He had just come off a retirement of several years and was in full support of the ADFPA.

As I had hoped, coaching Mike Bridges was a pleasure and an honor. What I hadn't anticipated is learning the lesson of self-control that he inadvertently taught me.

In powerlifting, each competitor has three attempts in each event, which are the squat, the bench press, and the deadlift. A competitor has to make one lift in each of the three events to secure a total. The lifter with the highest total is the winner, and those who do not complete one successful lift in each of the three contested categories are eliminated from the contest, regardless of how well they perform in the other two events.

As expected, Mike sailed through the squats, breaking Bill Schmidt's previous world record. He did the same in the bench press. Everything seemed so effortless, like he didn't try at all. After all, everyone else would yell, bark at the bar, sniff ammonia capsules, slap each other in the face, or do whatever they felt necessary to succeed. Mike did none of that, but squatted and benched like no one else could. He reached the third and final lift, the deadlift, with a commanding lead. Mike and I sat down to strategize the best plan for optimizing both his deadlift and total score.

We agreed that for his first attempt, he would take an opening weight that would be fairly conservative for him. We selected 622 pounds, which he crushed. In my eyes this was enough to put him way out of reach; he was a cinch to be the 1989 Drug Free World Champion. The only question was what else did he want to accomplish to make this event meaningful.

After assuring, reassuring, and reassuring again, Mike felt comfortable that the meet was out of reach for others. Then he said, "Tim, I want to deadlift 737, but that is over a 100 pound jump, and I am a little tired, and I know I'll have to go up there soon. I feel like I need more rest."

"Mike, correct me if I'm wrong, but that would be more than you have ever deadlifted in your life, at any time, in any organization. Am I right?"

"Yes, but I know I can do 737. I know that's the right weight. I don't think I could do more but I'm sure I can do that."

"You know," I said, "You are talking about deadlifting more weight than you, the great Mike Bridges, have ever lifted at any time in your career. You're a guy coming out of retirement. You haven't competed in years, and you're talking about out-pulling the best Bridges has ever pulled."

"Tim, I believe I can do it, but I'm afraid I can't today. I'll have to pull it in five minutes and I need more rest. I know I can do this. I'm just disappointed it won't work out that way."

With that in mind I devised a miracle plan for Mike Bridges. In my scenario, he would call for 737 pounds for his second attempt, but he would pass taking the lift. The weight would then be dropped down so other competitors could take their third lift. The meet would end with Mike asking for his third lift to be 737 pounds, only this time he would actually try it. This would give him the rest he needed, and the opportunity to do what he no one else imagined he could do: pull more weight than he had ever pulled in his life.

With no visible sign of emotion, Mike Bridges won a long hard battle against 737 pounds. I'll never forget the look on the face of Mike Lambert, the Powerlifting USA editor, who knows everything that has ever happened in the history of powerlifting. The lift took about ten seconds. Had he tried to deadlift 738 pounds that same day, he would have surely failed. World Champion Ray Benemerito passed the comment that had Bridges put more chalk on his hands for that lift, he would have failed.

Working with the best lifter in the history of the world was priceless. Never once did he yell, shove smelling salts up his nose, or bang his head on the bar, as many competitors did. He knew the exact weights to choose and sat in a somewhat unnerving, calm manner between lifts, a manner atypical for powerlifters.

I have been in this sport for thirty years and seen thousands of people approach it as though victory depended only on how much they could psych themselves up. Mike Bridges, with his calm, poised, in-complete-control approach, fascinated me. For years after meeting him, I have tried to teach athletes to stay inside their own heads, and not to look for outside sources to drive them. The contest just seems to always go to that one person who concentrates on themselves, not everything around them.

In their 1908 research studies, which were published in the Journal of Comparative Neurology and Psychology under the title, "The relation of strength of stimulus to rapidity of habit-formation," Robert M. Yerkes and J.D. Dodson showed that psyching yourself up too much causes a decline in performance. In my eyes, they could have saved themselves the research subjects and time by watching Mike Bridges.

From that day onward, I have understood why this quiet man has earned the right to be called Mike Bridges, "The Greatest Lifter in the History of the World." I only wish the thousands of other athletes I have coached since then, including many of the world's best, could have been with me to see the master of self control.

Plato said, "The greatest conquest of all lies within one's self." So did Bridges.

Mike Bridges over two decades later, and still the greatest.

Chapter 45

SHARING YOUR PASSION
FRED GLASS

"It's been said in sports you can never fully pay back those that have given their heart and their many hours to coach you. The way to payback, therefore, is to pay forward onto others."
- Unknown

Fred Glass was my first powerlifting coach. Powerlifting, as a sport, involves three lifts: the squat, the bench press, and the deadlift. Fred started coaching me in college, and though I didn't have great genetics for the sport, he managed to get results from me. Because of Fred, I won my first meet, in Harrisburg, Pennsylvania and I made all of the eight lifts I attempted. Years later, Fred and I coached a team of lifters together, a team that went on to win the American Drug Free Powerlifting Association's first National Championships among many other competitions.

Fred did about everything a competitor could possibly do. He went to local meets, regional meets, national meets, and World Championships. As a "master" lifter, a term given to those over forty years of age, he competed against the young guys as well as his own age group. In total, he has won sixteen World Championships in several age groups. Twice, he not only won the World Championships, but was named, pound for pound, the best lifter. He set over fifty world and national records along the way, sometimes in the squat, usually in the deadlift, and often with respect to the total of the three lifts. If he could have accomplished something more as a lifter, given that he is now in his early seventies, I cannot imagine what.

Despite his amazing career, the dozens of National and World

Championships and records, something makes Fred Glass stick out even further amongst his peers and competitors: his willingness to share his passion in his sport.

When I started powerlifting, Fred delivered cases of Pepsi as a day job, as in, he carried cases of Pepsi for 12 hours a day off a truck and into stores. We would then meet at seven thirty in the evening and lift until ten. Fred, only 123 pounds, got some five hours of sleep a night before throwing heavy cases of Pepsi for the twelve hours before our training session. His schedule never diminished his happiness. Nor did it stop him from inviting more and more people he barely knew into his tiny home basement gym in a row house in Allentown, Pennsylvania. He coached us with enthusiasm, teaching us to lift seriously heavy weights.

In the meantime, he attended every competition in Pennsylvania, New York, New Jersey, and Delaware. He competed five times a year and another ten or more times per year he would judge. At every meet he coached. I saw this man spend countless hours coaching people he had never met before, including younger kids that were stronger than he was, kids that were even in his own weight class. He never refused anyone help. He would drive guys from Pennsylvania to Chicago to compete, and he would also drive that far just to sit in a chair for ten

Rich Wenner (left), one of many champion powerlifters that has benefitted from time spent with Fred Glass.

hours to judge, a job that paid nothing. Fred Glass helped enable guys like Bill Schmidt, Joe Catalfamo, Todd VanBodegom-Smith, Jim Cope, Rich Wenner, and dozens of others to go on and achieve national acclaim. Fred was unlike so many others, who think only about their own performance, their own conquest of heavy weights, and their own trophy collection. Fred was there for others. He was there, all of the time, for others and was there for over four decades.

I wish every athlete I ever coached had the blessing of meeting Fred Glass. I know he touched hundreds of others, people who would share my sentiment that Fred Glass taught us by example that giving is better than receiving.

If you have a passion, share it.

Fred Glass winning yet another World Championship deadlifting 385 pounds at 72 years of age.

Chapter 46

FOR GIVING A KID A CHANCE
DON CLEMONS

"A hundred years from now it will not matter what my bank account was, the sort of house I lived in, or the kind of car I drove... but the world may be different because I was important in the life of a child."
  -Unknown

1983 photo of Don Clemons helping start my career as a strength and conditioning coach.

I believe that I am halfway through my career as a strength and conditioning coach. Even at this halfway mark, I've had a lifetime of amazing experiences. I've coached the fastest swimmer to ever enter the water, the top sumo wrestler in Japan, two World Champion Russian boxers, a track and field athlete who set over thirty National and World records, the highest paid player in the NFL, an NFL Hall of Fame member, All-Star baseball players and countless oddities from various sports. Without Don Clemons, I couldn't have accomplished any of this.

Halfway through my undergraduate education, I decided I wanted to do something more than just coach football, which was my original intention. Sure, football would have been a great occupation, but I wanted something more. At the time, I did competitive powerlifting. It dawned on me that if I became a strength and conditioning coach, I could have a direct impact on a football team's success and train other athletes as well.

I hoped the diversity of coaching athletes from many sports would challenge me. At the time, some major colleges were starting to hire full time strength coaches, but many did not. I knew that not many jobs existed, and to get one, I would have to do some pretty drastic things. It was quite a contrast to the present time, when most high schools employ a strength and conditioning coach.

I started by writing letters of inquiry to several major programs. Having been active in the in the field as an undergraduate, I expected a favorable response. Four of the five programs I wrote never replied at all. One, the granddaddy of them all, sent me a letter telling me they weren't interested in me, even as a volunteer assistant. I found this astounding. As an undergraduate, I had competed as a powerlifter, coached a very successful collegiate club team, coached various athletes in the weight room, and published about a dozen related articles. I would willingly move from home to volunteer my time, and my resume indicated success at all of the endeavors I had chosen, so I was quite surprised to read a letter that said I wouldn't be welcome even as a volunteer.

I contacted "Flip," my high school football coach, who had been a mentor to me. He suggested I contacted the Arizona State strength coach, Don Clemons. Like me, Don came from Lehigh Valley, and Flip spoke well of him. That same day I got an unrelated call from Doug Pollard, the head powerlifting coach of the National Champion Kutztown State College team. He mentioned Don Clemons' name as well. After a rejection letter and four major schools not bothering to respond, I had gotten the same lead twice in one day.

I flew out to interview with Don the summer before my senior year. Don lived up to his billing. Everybody I met back then liked Don Clemons, and to this day I've never heard anything different. Arizona appealed to me, since the school had great athletes and the weather was perfect.

That December, when I graduated, I moved into Don Clemon's apartment with $125 in my pocket and a promise that I could sleep on his floor for a week. A week turned into several months, and I managed to find part time jobs to support me so I could volunteer for Don Clemons. It wasn't easy. Moving three thousand miles from home, with no money, no transportation, and no friends was challenging. Thankfully I had one constant, a guy who was willing to give a kid a chance. Without that guy I have no idea where I would have ended up, but I truly believe it would have been nowhere close.

Because of Don Clemons, I have taken in many interns over the years. Most of them were lacking the experience they should have to work with the athletes I coach, but decades earlier, my life was changed because a man was willing to give a kid a chance, and he taught me to do the same. Thank you, "Big Daddy" Don. Your spirit has remained with me.

▲

Chapter 47

JUDGING TOO QUICKLY
CARDO URSO

"When you meet a man, you judge him by his appearance. When you leave a man, you judge him by his heart."
　-Russian Proverb

In the 1990s I pursued martial arts training pretty aggressively. Sensei Ray Hughes taught me karate and Sensei Christophe Leininger put me through judo and ju-jitsu hell training on a nightly basis. Andy Bauman, the Ja Shin Do instructor, put me through workouts that made hell seem like a tropical vacation in the Caribbean. I also played around with some full contact kickboxing. At the time, it seemed I was fighting everyone in the world except my wife. Workouts were long and intense and my body was continually beaten up.

During this period, my close training partner, Todd Milhoan, suggested we learn sombo techniques, sombo being a Russian martial art that had elements similar to judo, ju-jitsu, and wrestling. In this high-testosterone era, I willfully dived in. So we practiced sombo for an hour and a half each night before we even started judo.

In 1998, we attended the United States Sombo Association's National Championships in Washington D.C. Sombo requires competitors to wear shorts and a top resembling a judo gi, modified to look like the Russian military uniform. Competitors win by locking an opponent's arms and legs into a submission hold. The opponent must voluntarily tap out, acknowledging defeat, or risk having limbs dislocated through hyperextension or hyper-flexion. Competitors can also win by scoring points for various throws and takedowns, as in judo or wrestling. Because of the event's diversity, our small Phoenix team looked forward to testing our skills against the rest of the nation.

As is always the case in these events, opponents spend considerable time sizing each other up before the beginning of the event. And you can, if you want, watch every opponent during their warm-up and try to figure out their favorite techniques beforehand. I try not to do this. This probably isn't the smartest of strategies but I prefer the challenge of having to think and respond in the moment. This, to me, is the highest form of martial art training. I therefore dislike getting near the warm-up areas or hearing about other competitors, but the talk always seems to find me. At this meet, the other guys on the Phoenix team kept saying things to me like, "Look at this guy over here from the Marines. Can you believe the size of the arms on him?" Or, "I saw this guy doing lots of throws to warm up. He has killer throws." There was no shortage of commentary at this event. The man who was most talked about, as I later found out, was Cardo Urso.

Cardo Urso has the sort of presence that makes you believe in a supreme form of human being. His strength and discipline seem superhuman, and his military haircut makes him resemble Sergeant Carter, the volatile officer on the old "Gomer Pile" television series—only Urso doesn't have a moderate build. He looks as thick as a brick wall, and stronger. His seriousness only adds to the mystique.

As if looking at him didn't tell me enough, Todd told me he had earned fourteen different black belts, and was a Master Gunnery Sergeant, a tactical defense instructor for the United States Marine Corps, and very probably in my weight class. Thanks, Todd. Way to pump up your training partner.

A fight is a fight, and I was there to fight, so I put it out of my mind. I had a very physical first match against a stronger and younger competitor. I won, but found myself battered and heaving violently over the garbage can at the scorer's table. This went on for a good ten minutes. The human body is a funny thing, and so despite feeling sicker than I have ever felt, I somehow found an energy reserve a few minutes before my next fight. Out I went again. I needed every bit of physical and mental training I had ever gotten over decades of crazy Sensei's just to get through, but get through I did. Feeling proud and trashed, I went to the scorers table to see who I would be fighting. Why did it have to be Cardo Urso? He was the last guy I wanted to fight. I was already puking—without an opponent in front of me.

I entered the mat and saw a human pit-bull in front of me. I was about to face the human pit-bull myself. Plato said, "The greatest conquest is one's self," and I tried to overcome my thoughts about his size and discipline, his fourteen black belts, that he had been a tactical defense instructor for the Marine Corp, and his commanding presence. Looking at him, I thought he had to be the toughest and meanest man on earth. He was a villain, a bully, a monster, I thought.

When given the command to wrestle, competitors instantly fight to grip their opponent's jacket. My judo instructor, Christophe Leininger, demands all his students be great grip fighters, and so I had been trained well. I pride myself on my ability to force my opponent to let me grip as I want. I felt competent at that, at least, and so as we started to grip I thought I might be able to out-grip him. That took my mind off fighting the big bad man. Feeling his strength, though, snapped me back to reality. I had never felt this sort of strength before. I had wrestled Mark Coleman and Mark Kerr, the top two Ultimate Fighters in the world in the heavyweight division. I had trained with Dan "The Beast" Severn, who, back in his time, was also the top Ultimate Fighter. I had trained with several Olympic gold medalists, world champions, and national champions of freestyle wrestling. Yet I still had never felt anything like this guy before, even when training with those two hundred-sixty pound guys with no body fat. His grip felt like a vise and every time I tried to grip the jacket I might have been trying to grab a brick wall. I never imagined anyone that strong.

I was somehow fortunate enough to have won the match against Cardo

I was throughly impressed with Cardo Urso during our match, but became much more so when we had a chance to talk afterward.

Urso that day, but that isn't the important part of the story. The story begins when I had the chance to speak to him afterward. He fought like a champion, and though he did not win the championship that day, he represented himself like one. He came to congratulate me and offered his hand in friendship. We talked for the next half hour, and he caught me off guard by coming off as pleasant, mellow, caring, and intelligent. One minute I was fighting Godzilla, the next I was chatting amiably with Godzilla. I learned that Sergeant Urso loves his country and the men he teaches. He does everything in his power to instill in them the discipline and character they need to save their lives and protect their peers.

His undertaking is a noble calling and he does it exceptionally well. If asked to describe him before our match, I would have called him a pit bull. During the match, I would have called him Godzilla. But after our conversation, I would have used words like caring, understanding, forthright, and genuine.

Sergeant Urso taught me a lesson that day; he taught me not to judge a book by its cover. I had vilified this man as the meanest, toughest creature on the planet, and came to find out later he cared so much about his troops, and he has devoted his life to defending people like myself. Sergeant Urso taught me to keep reading the book, up until the end of the last chapter. Sergeant Urso, it was an honor to compete with you and a greater honor to learn from your example. I am sure I speak for thousands in saying thank you.

Chapter 48

POSITIVE REPRESENTATION
DAN O'BRIEN

"When you're half way up, you're always half way down."
-Celine Dion, from the song "Think Twice"

The world's greatest athlete Dan O'Brien (right) tutoring NFL quarterback John Beck .

In the late 1980s, the national decathlon program hosted a developmental seminar in Phoenix for the local up and coming decathletes. The world's foremost authority on the decathlon, Frank Zarnowski, attended to speak, evaluate talent, and help prospective Olympians. Fred Samara, a former Olympian himself and now a coach; Ed Gorman, a standout field event coach; and others came to assist. I was asked to provide strength and conditioning consultation to the athletes and staff and to help administer a weight room testing protocol.

The clinic was a several day affair, and a great deal of fun. Zarnowski gave me a copy of his recently published decathlon book, personally autographed. Coaches Samara and Gorman had fun-loving personalities and worked hard. The athletes were talented, young, and motivated. It was one of those times when we worked long and hard but it was so pleasurable that it didn't seem like work at all.

It has been almost two decades since that clinic, but I have thought back to it often throughout the years. When I do so, two athletes come to mind. One is a guy named Sheldon Blockburger, a great young decathlete from Louisiana State University. I remember him well because his test measures were off the charts. We measured vertical jump, long jump, power clean, bench press, pull-ups, and sit and reach flexibility test. He and one other guy significantly out performed everyone else in the field in every measure. That other guy was Dan O'Brien.

Like Sheldon, Dan stuck out in my mind because of his athletic ability, but that wasn't the main reason. The main reason Dan has remained in my memory banks is the way he represented himself. He was engaging, happy, and positive. He seemed to feel that every minute of life was thrilling. His enthusiasm was contagious, and marked him as different than most. He was the type of guy you just wanted to be around.

Several years later, Dan's career caught fire. He won a chain of World Championships in the decathlon. He also won the Goodwill Games and the 1996 Olympic Games in Atlanta. Along the way he set both world records and tied legendary Bill Toomey's record for number of wins of U.S. National Championships. I was thrilled to see him enjoy that kind of success. He was absolutely the kind of guy you would wish that on.

In 1999, Dan and I reunited. Dan had moved to Scottsdale, Arizona and was trying to make a comeback, despite some pretty serious injuries. Greg Hull, an extraordinary track coach himself, suggested Dan see me for strength training and he did. We worked together for several months and I marveled at how being named the world's best athlete—the title given to the man who sets the world record in the decathlon—had not changed him at all. He had gone from being a clinic attendee to the world's top athlete, and he was the same old guy, with impossible enthusiasm and energy. Dan's injuries and travels eventually forced him to retire and took him away from our training environment. I lost touch with him.

Years later, Dan called me and we agreed to meet at Arizona Track and Cross Country Coach's annual seminar, where we were both speaking. We met for an hour or so between our talks. Again, Dan amazed me by seeming thrilled with every moment of life, though we were merely sitting around catching up. I saw him go from wanna-be kid out of college, to the best in the world, to a guy with severe injuries, to someone retired from the sport. But always constant, Dan O'Brien remained that youthful, energetic, outgoing guy.

A few years later, I trained Brigham Young University's star quarterback, John Beck, for the NFL Scouting Combine. I had worked with John since high school days and knew his whole family well. John's father, Wendell, asked if I could arrange for John to do speed training with an elite track coach. I knew just who to call: Dan O'Brien. Dan not only knows track on a world class level, but he has done it and done it well. With Dan's personality and love for others, I knew he would be the perfect fit. He was.

I don't think that dropping Dan behind enemy lines in the middle of a war could change his outlook or demeanor. If I were in a war, stuck in a proverbial foxhole, I would want him there with me; I could count on him to have the right attitude. In the song "Think Twice," Celine Dion sings, "When you're halfway up, you're always halfway down." I've seen a lot of Dan, and he's never halfway down. I love that about Dan O'Brien. He has always represented himself as a helpful, caring, happy, positive guy. Perhaps he's the world's greatest at that as well.

Chapter 49

HANDLING PRESSURE
RIA STALMAN

"To be under pressure is inescapable. Pressure takes place through all the world: war, siege, the worries of state. We all know men who grumble under these pressures, and complain. They are cowards. They lack splendor. But there is another sort of man who is under the same pressure, but does not complain. For it is the friction which polishes him. It is pressure which refines and makes him noble."

-St. Augustine

In the early 1980s, the Arizona State University football weight room had an electric atmosphere. Don "Big Daddy" Clemons, ASU's football strength and conditioning coach, ran the place. The facility was meant to be used by football players only, but Don had a way of caring for any athletes who were sincere about their training.

The football teams were powerhouses then, stuffed with All-American players like Vernon Maxwell, Mike Richardson, and Jim Jeffcoat. Other high-profile athletes who used the facility included All-American baseball players, Barry Bonds and Oddibe McDowell; future Olympic gold medalist in the 4x100 meter relay, Ron Brown; future NBA standout player and coach, Bryon Scott; 600 pound bench presser and track athlete, Gary Willicky, who led the world in the shot-put with a throw of 68 feet and 2 inches. Nevertheless, this story is about the American record holder in discus, Leslie Deniz, and Leslie's training partner and competitive rival, Ria Stalman of Holland.

At the time, Leslie held the American record, but Ria's best was just a bit better than Leslie's. Often, when two great athletes are thrown together, both of their performances improve. I saw this scenario play out both on the track and in the ASU weight room. I wasn't training them, but I did help them out in the weight room from time to time. Ria had just started to peak in both her strength lifts and discus throws and had difficulty making gains. When athletes get to that place—when they've just about maximized their physiological potential—they struggle to make even small gains, a source of endless frustration. Ria had reached that place.

Leslie, on the other hand, was an "up and comer." Though stronger than Ria, she had not yet come as close to her physical peak, and so she made consistent gains. Ria would come to the weight room, excited about bench pressing 290 pounds five times. Leslie would come in—as they often trained together—and bench press 300 pounds five times. Ria would bust her butt weeks later and make 295 pounds five times. Leslie would manage 310. This went on until Ria bench pressed an astonishing 325 pounds five times. At the time, competitive powerlifters did not wear the support shirts designed for bench pressing, which add up to 100 pounds to someone's lifting ability. They wore standard T-shirts. Also, at the time, the most weight any female anywhere on the planet had ever bench pressed in competition was 335 pounds one time.

Ria's lift showed her capable of more than any woman in the history of the world, but she was a discus thrower, not a powerlifter, and she was six months away from the 1984 Olympic Games. A training partner like Leslie must have been a blessing for Ria, pushing her to greater heights, but also putting almost unbearable pressure on her; every time Ria would do something amazing, like bench press 325 pounds, Leslie would top it. When I say top it, I mean, TOP IT. Leslie went on to bench press an unthinkable 360 pounds. Not only did she bench 360 pounds, but she did it five times. I know, because I spotted her when she did it.

This didn't apply only to bench presses. Ria would power-clean 300 pounds three times, and Leslie would power-clean 315 pounds three times. Ria would half-squat 475 pounds five times, and Leslie would half-squat 570, four times.

The big day finally came—the Olympic Games, and not surprisingly, both Leslie and Ria made the women's discus finals. Ria entered with a further lifetime best mark, but Leslie was breaking both the American discus and weight room records every time she tried. The day of the finals was no exception. Leslie led through the first five throws. She was one mere throw away from winning the Olympic gold medal. I imagine Ria's thought process to be something like this. "I just don't have it today. Leslie has been on fire, and she's on fire today. This is a bad day to not be my best. I've gone through four years of training, and there's only one throw left, and I just can't seem to catch her." Ria had devoted every minute of every day for four years to the discus, and seemed about to be beaten by someone that she probably could have beaten, since Ria did have a better lifetime best mark. There was only one throw left, perhaps the last throw Ria Stalman would ever take in her life. This throw would forever distinguish her as someone who won a gold medal, or someone who should have won a gold medal, but didn't.

Ria Stalman won the gold medal that day. She overtook Leslie on her very last throw, throwing 65.36 meters. She could have succumbed to the pressure for a lot of reasons, and I saw those reasons almost daily for the twelve months leading up to the Olympics. Ria Stalman never gave in. In fact, when the pressure was the greatest, Ria was at her greatest.

I've often thought that if this lovely woman can handle so much, I can handle the little difficulties that crop up in daily life. Thank you, Ria, for being a shining example of how to handle immense pressure. Your picture has been on my wall for over twenty years now, to remind me. I feel blessed to work with both ladies, who have always been happy, kind, and courteous around me. It's too bad they couldn't both win Olympic gold that day. They both deserved the medals as discus throwers and as compassionate human beings.

181

Chapter 50

TAKING THE FIRST STEP
JOE CATALFAMO

"The journey of a thousand miles begins with the first step."
   -Anonymous

Drug-Free World Champion, Junior World Champion, National
Champion, Collegiate National Champion, and multiple record
holder, Joe Catalfamo.

Growing up in Allentown, Pennsylvania afforded me exposure to some serious blue-collar work ethic in the weightroom. My brother Keith introduced me to weights at a very young age, when he was training for high school football. Years later, my high school coach Tom Filipovits poured gas on my fire, at a time when I was attempting to better my own high school football career. In college I met the immortal Fred Glass, a multiple National and World Champion who seemed to exist only to powerlift. He infected me with his love for heavy squats, bench presses, and deadlifts. I got hooked on powerlifting.

In my junior year at East Stroudsburg State College (now East Stroudsburg University), my training partners and I decided to form the school's first-ever competitive powerlifting team. We approached anyone we saw in the weight-room of above average strength, and put ads in the school newspaper, "The Stroud Courier."

Weight classes range from 114 pounds to super heavy weight. There are few strong college-aged males under 165 pounds, so we especially targeted anyone interested who could compete in the 114, 123, 132 and 148 pound classes. Since these classes probably wouldn't fill, just having a representative would earn the team points. A proficient lifter would be like a double bonus.

One Tuesday night, three of us were training in what may have been the worst collegiate weightroom of all time. A small, mustached, Italian-looking guy walked up to us and said, "I'm Joe." Then he stopped talking and stared at us.

Tuesday night meant heavy squats, and so we were busy. We loaded on plate after plate, wrapped our knees, chalked our hands and backs, and inhaled smelling salts to psych ourselves up before and during the lift. With all the commotion we forgot about Joe. Then Todd Van Bodegom-Smith (real name, not an alias) said, "Hey Mac, who's the guy in the corner?"

"I don't know. Some guy, said his name is Joe. I thought he might be here to see you guys. He didn't say anything else to me," I said.

"Mac, maybe he wants to powerlift," Todd said. I went on a bit of a tirade after that, no doubt fueled by the electricity in the air and the aggression that accompanies squats. No way this guy came to powerlift. He would have said something. He certainly had plenty of opportunity.

After some prodding from Todd and others, I asked the quiet guy if he wanted to powerlift. He said "yes," and nothing else. I wondered what had gone wrong with this guy and what planet he came from. He wouldn't talk and he seemed so disinterested. Nevertheless, I sent him to the corner to do three sets of ten repetitions of squats, bench presses, and deadlifts with a forty-five pound bar. The guy looked at me as though I was crazy, as if he were offended that I had asked him to actually do something. I think every fourteen-year-old female enrolled in a basic weight-training class in high schools throughout the country can lift more than this, so it wasn't as if I had asked him to move mountains. Perhaps Joe was good for more, but he seemed so quiet and disinterested that I didn't want to push it.

Interesting enough, Joe came back three times a week for the next month. He didn't seem to like us, and didn't talk to us, but he weighed only 111 pounds and he didn't bother us much. We figured if we ever actually got this guy to a contest we might actually get some team points out of him.

Two months later, in late November, was the first contest, the Wyoming Valley Open. We decided to leave from college and car-pool together that morning, so that we'd get there in time for early weigh-ins. We asked Joe to go with us. He mumbled that he would rather just meet us there. We knew what that meant: he would be a no-show.

To our surprise, Joe showed up. Not only did he show up, but he did a 200 pound squat, 145 pound bench press, and 320 pound deadlift, for a second place finish. Who would have ever guessed?

Upon leaving, the other East Stroudsburg team members and I made plans to compete the following weekend in Glasboro, New Jersey. We never asked Joe, because he still didn't seem to like us, and he still didn't seem interested. When we concluded the plans we started to disband, and that time Joe actually initiated his first conversation with us.

"There's a meet at Glasboro next week. I think you guys are all going to it. I want to go to it too. I think I can qualify for the collegiate nationals," he said.

"How did you know this, and why do you want to go?" I asked.

"I heard the cute girl, Gerri Ellingsworth, in my weight class mention it, and you guys seem like you want to go. I want to get good at this and feel if I can just take the first step I can make being good at this happen."

The next week, Joe Catalfamo qualified for the collegiate nationals in Glasboro, New Jersey. Within a year, his combined total went from 665 pounds to 815 pounds. Within a few years he had become a collegiate All-American, a multiple time Collegiate National Champion, a Collegiate National record holder, a Junior World Champion, an Open National Champion, a men's American record-holder, and a Drug-free World Champion. As a 114 pound lifter who had never touched performance enhancement drugs, Joe squatted 407 pounds, bench pressed 265 pounds and deadlifted 440 pounds.

At some point, Joe's father came to me and thanked me for helping Joe. He said that Joe had grown up small, quiet, and shy, and that he prayed Joe would find something in college to succeed at. Joe's success at powerlifting far exceeded those prayers. He said he never dreamed his quiet kid would become a World Champion. On that day, I had a new understanding of the day Joe Catalfamo and I met. Simply put, he was just shy.

Needless to say, years of traveling all over the country with Joe gave me an opportunity to find out what a wonderful person he was on the inside. Once shy around me, he became a dear friend, someone I know I can count on to this very day, and someone who taught me a valuable lesson: the first step. Taking the first awkward step.

If you are willing to take the first step, and follow it up with subsequent steps, you may just be able to transform yourself from a guy who barely speaks into something great, like the sort of person who wins World Championships. Joe, we helped each other to become better. Thank you.

Chapter 51

FRIENDSHIP
"ALICIA-SAN" AND "MISS EMILY"

"Friendship is one mind in two bodies."
        -Mencius

Inseparable friends: Emily Adams and Alicia Robinson
All photos courtesy of Alicia Robinson.

I met Alicia Robinson many years ago, when she was in high school. Alicia is the daughter of former NBA star Leonard "Truck" Robinson, and was earning quite the reputation for herself as a volleyball player. It wasn't hard to see why. She had great genes, an abundance of strength, and gave the impression she could spike a volleyball through a brick wall. Alicia loved to train and was as fun to be around as any kid I have ever worked with. To know her is to love her.

One day, the *Arizona Republic* newspaper in Phoenix ran a huge two-part article in the sports page about daughters of former NBA stars that had excelled in volleyball. One part was about Alicia Robinson. It was a huge article and beautifully done. The other was about Emily Adams, daughter of former Phoenix Suns great Alvan Adams. I had never met Emily, so when I cut out the article to hang on the bulletin board, I kept Alicia's article and tossed the rest. I was mortified the next day when Emily Adams showed up and saw our bulletin board, and recognized that Alicia's picture was up and hers was not. I wondered if she would be hurt enough not to return.

Thankfully, Emily Adams came back to train with me. Like Alicia, Emily is the sort of person I would want to be around twenty-four hours a day. She is courteous, caring, and her intellect is off the charts. Emily wasn't hurt that I'd tossed out her picture. Interestingly, Alicia was.

I found out Alicia and Emily were best friends. They did everything together. They knew each other so well that at times, they seemed to function like an old married couple. While Emily was smart enough to recognize that I didn't know her at the time I hung Alicia's picture, Alicia didn't want to be up there without Emily for fear of hurting her best friend.

I have coached thousands of teenage females, and I've seen many of them with their best friends, but I've never seen a pair of friends as close as these two. There isn't anything they wouldn't do to help one another. And it wasn't just a one year high-school fad.

Alicia and Emily attended the University of Southern California together on volleyball scholarships; they went as a package deal. They lived together. They both had significant playing time their freshman year and went on to lead the team to National Collegiate Athletic Association's National Championship twice in their three years as starters. The summer after their first NCAA Championship, they both came home to train. One morning, Alicia approached me and said, "Tim, you've given almost everybody a nickname  except for me. I need a nickname. I think from now on I want to be Alicia-san, so I'm like Hanada-san." Alicia was making reference to perhaps the greatest sumo wrestler of all time, Masaru Hanada, whom we called Hanada-san out of respect, and in accordance with Japanese etiquette. So Alicia, of the dynamic duo, became Alicia-San.

Later that day, with no knowledge of my conversation with Alicia, Emily Adams came in and informed me she thought she was one of the only ones whom I hadn't given a nickname. Emily always called me "Mr. Tim," in reference to the way future New York Knick star Channing Frye addressed me. At the time, Channing was in high school and as great a kid as you could imagine. With deep-rooted manners, Channing would call me nothing but "Mr. Tim," the

way his parents taught him. With Emily Adams being about three times as smart as a normal kid, she picked right up on it. She called me "Mr. Tim," affectionately, playfully. Thus, that same day that Alicia became Alicia-san, Emily became Miss Emily. That the girls had the same thought on the same day didn't surprise me; they seemed to function as one mind in two bodies.

College came and went for the athletes. One of them always stayed in contact with me. One semester it would be Alicia-san. The next, it would be Miss Emily. They never discussed this and it was not planned. They would never both be in touch with me during the same semester, but one of them always called, sent E-mails, and brought back a full compliment of photographs. I felt as though I had attended their every game, experienced all of their parties, knew their boyfriends well, attended their awards banquets, and had fun on their volleyball team trips. About half of the photographs would have both girls in them, and they always looked happy.

After graduation, Alicia lived in Phoenix for a while, before moving to Los Angeles with her boyfriend Chauncey. Emily stayed in Los Angeles and then went to play professionally in Puerto Rico. When she retired from professional volleyball, she moved back to Phoenix, and then to Atlanta. Life took them in different directions, but their friendship never changed. They were the same inseparable friends they had always been despite the thousands of miles stretched between them.

It has dawned on me, after watching these two for so many years, that they have an amazing built-in system. They each have someone to look out for them. When one needs to make a decision, she has two brains instead of one. Their continual support for one another seems to make them both twice as happy and twice as successful as a normal person. As wonderful as they each are individually, this one plus one friendship always equates to three, or four, or even more. My heart always feels warm around these two, and their never-ending lesson is one I will never forget.

TIME MANAGEMENT FOR EDUCATION
MARTY ALVAREZ

"An investment in knowledge always pays the best interest."
  -Benjamin Franklin

Marty Alvarez (right) with training partner and friend Sergei Sheydayi.

Unlike several others written about in this book, Marty Alvarez is not a world-class athlete. Yes, he has had his black belt in Shotokan karate for over twenty years, but he has never aspired to be a high-level competitive fighter. Instead, he practices for two more noble endeavors: personal growth and to teach others. Marty Alvarez is, however, world class—a world class person and a world class builder. A co-owner of Sun Eagle Corporation, Arizona's "premier construction management company," he is on the go every waking hour.

The lesson I learned from Marty is how to get a free education, the easy way. After training one day, I mentioned to a mutual training partner, Sergei Sheydayi, I was tired of listening to the radio during commutes. I told him I had heard "Stairway to Heaven" and "Jumpin Jack Flash" too many times and I was getting bored with "Sweet Home Alabama." He mentioned that I should talk to Marty Alvarez because Marty is in the car non-stop and might have a good idea for me.

I found that Marty drives between 40,000 and 50,000 miles per year, all locally. He told me he listens to books on CD instead of the radio. I told him I had listened to one years ago and enjoyed it. He told me he had listened to over 900, and had been doing it for almost thirty years. Better yet, he signed them out of libraries, so he had the knowledge and wisdom of over 900 books inside of him and hadn't paid for any of it. Best of all, he did this during wasted commute time, when others were hearing the same song for the two hundredth time.

Nine hundred books. The wisdom of nine hundred books, free, during spare time. That lesson changed my life. Since that conversation with Marty, I've heard John Wooden, Donald Trump, Stephen Covey, Tony Robbins, Jim Collins, and all of the best that audio books have to offer. Indeed, this is world class wisdom I received from a world class man. Thank you Marty Alvarez.

Chapter 53

CREATING FRIENDSHIPS
TARA O'KEEFFE

"The only way to have a friend is to be one."
-Ralph Waldo Emerson

Fourteen-year old Tara O'Keeffe (center) after receiving a gold medal at a karate tournament.

In the early 1990s I was preparing to take my black belt exam in Wado-Ryu karate. The test was nine months away, but I knew I'd need that full amount of time to get myself through. Sensei Ray Hughes conducted the exam, and I found him to be the meanest Sensei on earth at that time. Sensei Marlon Moore, a perfectionist embodying the spirit of a true martial artist, scored the test as well. The test was comprised of three separate parts: fundamentals, technical components of both basic movements and fighting applications, and the spirit exam. They held one exam per day, and each lasted three hours. Previous test takers told me the three parts could be better classified as the pain exam, the pain exam, and the pain exam. To my knowledge, no one in that Wado system had ever passed their black belt exam on the first try, so testees who failed went through the three pain exams again. One testee, a talented and tough athlete, took the tests four times before passing.

So at the nine month mark prior to my test, I started adding extra work to my regimen. I was already doing martial arts six days per week, often two class sessions in one night. I lifted weights four times a week, but knew this program wasn't enough to get me through the test coming my way like a freight train.

I started running the mountain behind Sun Devil Stadium, timing every repetition. Three courses led to the top, and depending on the course, runs took three to five minutes of pure hell. I encouraged friends and athletes I coached to run with me. Many vomited, a by-product of the amount of lactic acid that circulated through their blood due to the extreme exertion of running the steep mountain.

I also spent extra time at the end of Sensei Ray's advanced training classes, which was no easy feat. At the end of many classes, most of the students lay on the bleachers unable to move. His classes were physically and mentally exhausting and he expected utter perfection of us. If so much as an eyebrow hair were out of place during a technique, Sensei Ray reprimanded us and demanded we repeat the technique over and over.

After these classes I fueled up on Gatorade and then headed back to the floor, on my own, in the true spirit of the samurai warrior. I hoped that would separate me from others who had taken or would take their black belt exam. After a month of self-imposed jigoku-kego ("hell training"), a young green belt girl, Tara, approached me.

"May I stay after class and train with you?" Tara asked.

"Do you know what I do in these workouts?"

"Yes," she said.

"Well let me tell you just to make sure. I am doing ten katas [pre-arranged movement sequences] after each class. Five of those will be Kushanku [an extremely long and especially difficult pattern.] After each of the ten katas I will be doing twenty-five push-ups on my knuckles. There will be no rest. You will have to do everything I do, with the same intensity. There will be no complaining, no negativity, and no quitting. Do you still want to do this?"

"Yes," she said.

I did this program for several months, with Tara at my side every step of the way. Dumbfounded as to why she would train this hard with me for such a long period of time, I finally broke down after class one night to ask her why she did all of this.

"Tara, why would you want to go through this when you're not the one testing for black belt?" I asked.

"Because I thought it would help you."

In a million years I would not have predicted that reply. I did not know this girl well and cannot imagine anyone, let alone a teenage girl, would be willing to go through that kind of pain to help out someone else.

Tara O'Keeffe went through those months, side by side with me, and her presence helped me to push myself. That, in addition to Sensei Ray's training, helped her become an accomplished black belt in her own right, some years later. I helped train her for that black belt exam. I stayed after class to help her, and ran the mountain behind Sun Devil Stadium with her. That kid I barely knew created a friendship with me I will always cherish. Since then, I've seen her grow up to graduate high school and college, earn her doctoral degree in physical therapy, marry and become a mother. This once sweet kid, willing to go through jigoku-kego to help me out, created a friendship to last a lifetime.

▲

Chapter 54

PROFESSIONALISM
JUDE LACAVA

"If asked to lay bricks, one ought to be the best brick layer he can be."
-Unknown

Sportscaster Jude LaCava
with former Diamondbacks
Coach Bob Brenly.

Anyone who has spent significant time in Phoenix, Arizona probably recognizes the name Jude LaCava. Jude is the very popular sportscaster for FOX 10 in Phoenix. A Sunday night in Phoenix wouldn't be the same without hearing, "FOX 10 sports with Jude LaCava coming up next." Consistently having a likeable professional broadcasting is comforting.

Twenty years ago, I had the pleasure of meeting Jude professionally, as he periodically came to Arizona State University for stories on the athletics program. I remember him as being fun yet courteous, sincere, and always professional. It wasn't hard to see that Jude was a loyal and passionate employee who was going to give FOX 10 sports their money's worth. His caring and sincerity seemed to make those he interviewed comfortable and more willing to share. In a town with many television stations and many good sportscasters, he established himself as the cream of the crop.

After I left ASU and went into private practice, years passed before I saw Jude again. Naturally, I was happy to see him, as he was someone I had fond memories of. I was pleased to reunite with someone who had grown up in the same blue-collar part of Pennsylvania as I had. We had a common background, and I knew it wouldn't be long before he reminded me that his high school, Salisbury, had beaten mine, Parkland, in basketball his senior year for the league championship. As if cued, Jude did so.

At this reunion, I offered to train Jude, and he accepted. I had the opportunity to see him as passionate and professional as he was in his younger days. Best of all, he served as a role model to me in terms of professionalism. Jude speaks only of the good traits of the athletes he covers, never disclosing confidentialities, criticizing, or passing judgment. He has never once interrupted the workouts of the professional and elite amateur athletes he trains beside daily, and he shows them the utmost respect. Most of them have commented to me that they appreciate him as a friend in the gym and not just another reporter out for a scoop.

I'm not sure if someone taught Jude LaCava this level of professionalism, or if he just has an extraordinary sense of propriety. I only know that Jude is a lovable, kind, and happy friend who I would do anything for. Anyone he interviews feels comfortable with him and he is always happy. The athletes he trains beside have the utmost respect for him. He simply out works others in his field and does it to perfection. With Jude LaCava, it is always a win-win situation. If only there were more people like him…

▲

Chapter 55

THE HUMBLE LEGEND
BOBBY ORR

"Humility is the solid foundation of all the virtues."
 -Confucius

Bobby Orr, the legend, (far right) with Dan LaCouture and myself

Bobby Orr may be the greatest hockey player ever to live. In an era when defensemen rarely scored at all, Bobby Orr won the 1969-70 and 1974-75 Art Ross Trophies, the annual award given to the leading scorer in the National Hockey League (NHL). To date, no other defenseman has ever earned that distinction. Bobby Orr revolutionized the game of hockey. Defensemen still study and imitate his techniques.

In the late 1990s I spent a summer in Boston helping train the off-ice strength and conditioning practices of hockey players. The players ranged from young teens to the elite pros of the Boston Bruins to a number of NHL players from other teams. Among the NHL players I worked with directly were Dan LaCouture, Tom Poti and Chris Drury, the former collegiate Hoby Baker Award winner.

Toward the end of the summer, Dan LaCouture asked me if I would be willing to meet with Bobby Orr, his agent. I thought he was kidding. Bobby Orr had been a childhood idol of mine. When we were kids, playing makeshift hockey games on the frozen ponds in Pennsylvania, we would always select pro players to represent. There were times when we all wanted to be Bobby Orr, and sometimes fights would break out over who would get the honor. Now I was being asked if I would be willing to meet him.

"Lac, I'd walk the 15 miles to his office and I'd drag my tongue on the ground every inch of the way if I had to, in order to meet Bobby Orr. Are you messing with me?"

"No, Mac," he said. "Tommy and I and a bunch of the guys have told him really good things about you and he wanted to meet you to talk about the possibility of doing business in the future."

I was thrilled. Dan called and set up an appointment and we met three days later.

I'm not sure exactly what I was expecting, but here was the guy who had changed the entire game—perhaps the only one in my lifetime that will ever do so in any game—and I felt no airs. The first thing Bobby Orr said was, "Tim, thank you for taking the time to meet with me. It's a pleasure to meet you. I hope you don't mind taking the time." I sat in amazement, not over the stature of the man, or his previous performances or his reputation. Rather, I was in awe because this guy, who was such an unbelievable hockey player, was also such an unbelievable person. The guy who changed the complexion of a whole game was telling me, the peon strength coach, how happy he was to be able to meet me. Talk about role reversal. Talk about a peon strength coach in shock.

For an hour and a half we talked. We talked business, and about clients of his whom I also worked with. We talked about his bad knees. I told him the story about "being" Bobby Orr on the frozen pond in Pennsylvania, and he cracked up. I was in awe that this famous hockey player could be so down to earth as a person. It was just a bunch of real guys living a real existence. The legend was one of us, and it could not have been more enjoyable.

No business materialized from that meeting, but over a decade later as I think about it I still kind of wish something will. If the premise of the movie "The Secret," is correct, and a person attracts things by dwelling on them, then I may just have to start envisioning a second meeting and/or a business deal with Bobby Orr. The first one was so good it left me ready for a sequel. Bobby, if you ever read this, give me a call. I have no doubt you are still unbelievable, and always will be. Learning that a legend could be so humble was an incredible experience for me, one I wish everyone could experience.

▲

Chapter 56

ACTIONS SPEAK LOUDER THAN WORDS
THE UNKNOWN SENSEI

"What you do speaks so loud that I cannot hear what you say."
  -Ralph Waldo Emerson

I honestly believe I can affect positive change in any athlete's physiology, anywhere in the world. Changing physiology is easy. Changing the mentality of an athlete requires far more work, but in my experience, engenders far more significant change in performance. During the past three decades, I've settled on a definitive set of principles, or core values, that I try to instill in every athlete.

One of the more unusual principals I teach athletes is to not talk about their performance. If they have performed well, we all know that, and strutting around bragging is not necessary. If they performed poorly, they know it and we saw it, and excuses and justifications are unnecessary. I learned this lesson fifteen years ago, from a man whose path crossed mine for exactly two hours. To this day I do not know his name, and probably never will.

In the early 1990s, I was Arizona State University's strength and conditioning coach. The football team had an away game scheduled against the University of Nebraska. I had no coaching responsibilities the Friday night before the game, and I saw this as a great opportunity to take a gi (training uniform) and find a different dojo to do some good training in. I often do this when I travel.

I ended up at Okinawan Goju Ryu karate school. I had never done an Okinawan art, or any Goju Ryu for that matter. Nevertheless, I practiced the Japanese martial art Wado Ryu, and thought the training would strengthen me as a karate practitioner. I asked if they accepted outside guests and they said yes.

I took a cab to the dojo and found myself there forty-five minutes before class. I always like to be early for martial art workouts and know that under the code of bushido, my actions reflect not only myself, but also my art and my sensei. I am obligated to be courteous, hard working, and humble.

As I sat waiting, an older gentleman with short white hair entered the dojo and sat down with me. I guessed him to be sixty-five. We chatted for a bit, and then long pauses filled our conversation. Unsure of what to do, I asked him what rank he had attained. From his appearance, I suspected him to be one of those guys in his mid sixties who was a novice or intermediate—one of those guys who needed a hobby and decided to try martial arts. Most times, those guys never become proficient, due to the difficulty of learning such complex motor skills so late.

"We're taught not to talk about such things," he said. "Those of high rank can be seen as pompous or bragging. Those of lower rank can be viewed as less important, and that's not really the case. The important issue is that we are all students, and we are all trying to grow. Isn't that your case?"

"Absolutely," I said. He was right, and I liked both what he said and how he said it. With that, the white haired old man pointed out the locker room and told me I was welcome to change back there and stretch before class.

I headed back to the locker room, changed into my gi, and spent the next fifteen minutes on a mat stretching. At that point I heard an authoritative voice yell, "Line up." Like the other students, I ran to my spot on the training floor for the formal bowing process. I was curious to see the sensei, since the only people I had seen before class were the old man and the students I stretched with. Then it hit me. The humble, white haired man who had taught me the lesson before class actually was the sensei. He had every right to talk about rank and yet didn't. He merely helped me become a better person and a better student that night. His actions spoke louder than his words ever could have.

I later found out he wasn't Roseberry Sho Rei Shobu Kan dojo's head instructor. Sensei Roseberry was out of town, leaving this wonderful student in charge for the evening. I will never forget the lesson he taught me before class had even started, and although I never got to know his name, I will never forget him.

Chapter 57

THE GIFT OF YOURSELF
GRIFFIN GOSNELL

"If there be any truer measure of a man than by what he does, it must be by what he gives."
　　-Robert South

Griffin Gosnell (left)
with sister Greer

　　Griffin Gosnell, who was 15 when I met her (and now a college student), is the sort of person who seems to give off energy. She was a pretty girl, slight of frame, with a nice athletic figure, a big quick smile, and impossibly beautiful long brown hair. There was no mistaking that hair. That hair could have been featured in a shampoo commercial.

　　Griffin came in to train one day with much of that beautiful hair missing.

"Griffin, you've had your hair cut," I said, a bit horrified.

"I donated it."

"You donated it? That must have been a tough decision to make, especially with your hair being as pretty as it is," I said.

"No. Now somebody else can enjoy it," she said. "It's much more important to me that some poor child enjoy that hair than that I do."

Nothing else needs to be said. Griffin Gosnell was willing to give up the most conspicuous element of her beauty to please someone she'd never even met. Her actions had said it all. The sacrifice was made, the good deed done, and the lesson learned.

Griffin, with your personality and spirit, you'd still be beautiful without any hair at all.

Chapter 58

TEAMMATES
MY TEAM

"True team spirit is a genuine consideration for others, an eagerness to sacrifice personal interest or glory for the welfare of the team."
    -John Wooden

2007 I.S.K.F. Western Region team: Meyer, Diouff, Ekrissin, Du, McClellan

I've always enjoyed examining the fine line that separates winning from losing in athletics. I have had the opportunity to study some of the world's best competitors in individual sports, including track and field, boxing, tennis, wrestling, and others. I'm always intrigued to observe the physical and mental factors that separate athletic success from failure.

Even more intriguing is the study of teams. Sometimes teams with little talent outperform those with great talent. Figuring out how this happens takes up many hours of my time and are some of the most intellectually stimulating hours of my life. Team competition, to me, is much more than trying to optimize the performance of each individual. A certain mentality and chemistry must be cultivated in individuals to optimize a team's performance. This is obviously a greater challenge and one I like to accept, as it puts me a bit more on edge.

In 2007, I captained the International Shotokan Karate Federation's Western Region team. For the previous twenty-three years, the Western Region's men's black belt team was pretty much a doormat for the rest of the country. In fact, in more than two decades, they had not once won the National Championship. In my eyes, as captain, winning the National Championship was the only goal. But, as the Western Region had been so bad, I knew it would be tough to pull off.

Madieyna Diouf, the top performer on the team, came from Senegal, Africa. What an amazing athlete he is. As 2007 Western States karate champion and 3rd degree black belt, Jeff Dodge, says: "I've never seen anybody jump across the room like him. He's got great technical skills and his athleticism is simply amazing. Watching him is like watching scenes from the movie "Crouching Tiger, Hidden Dragon." Had he grown up in the United States, his athleticism would have no doubt led him to become a stand-out defensive back in the NFL, making millions of dollars per year. Growing up in Africa, he never got that chance. Instead, he spent many hours every day learning to be a world class karate athlete. In his prime he was as good as anybody in the whole world. In my eyes, he was a sure victory for our team.

Simeon Ekrisson grew up on the Ivory Coast in Africa. Like Madieyna Diouf, he has exceptional speed. He is a highly successful competitor because of his intense energy and desire to train long and hard. He is a stand-out performer, training partner, and teacher. He has been a seven-time Grand Canyon Games State Champion and for years always placed in the top four in individual men's black belt competition at the ISKF Nationals. This year, I thought, would be no different. Like Diouf, he would certainly win.

Mark Meyer took to karate at a young age. He won almost every tournament there is to win. He has also directed tournaments, opened his own dojo, and taught students for more than a decade. Timing is a critical component that determines a fighter's success or failure. Mark Meyer has impeccable timing.

Every team seems to have a guy who isn't the most naturally talented but who achieves amazing results solely because of his efforts and desire. Mark Meyer was that guy for us. I felt confident he would win for us in each of his matches, because he seemed to win most all of his matches for the past decade. It did not matter who stood in front of him.

Jihone Du

Jihone Du, the fourth fighter in the lineup, would have been the top fighter on many teams. Jihone is fast, has practiced diligently for almost twenty years, and may be the smartest fighter in the entire Shotokan style. His exceptional talent and speed would be too much for opponents on the other team, I thought.

I was the fifth fighter on the team. Although I am far less talented than my teammates, I knew I had potential to beat some of the others who would fight in the National Championships. If things went well, we could possibly win all five matches against other teams, though we only needed three to win and advance to the next round. I think we all felt this could happen.

Unfortunately, it did not. Our team lost in the first round and had to fight back to place third. It was the same result as always.

Over the next two weeks, I dwelled upon how this very talented team fell into the same fate the Western Region always fell into—losing. I kept asking myself how I could put together a lineup of stars, a virtual who's who of Shotokan Karate, and have the same old fate. The answer grew clearer and clearer. I had put together a group of stars and not a team. We all pulled together, but functioned much the way the American Major League baseball stars, the USA Olympic Basketball "Dream Team" and U.S. 4x100 meter sprint teams have at times, as a bunch of stars that could not pull off winning as a team.

I vowed 2008 would be different. We assembled a team and started training the first day of January. Unfortunately, my respected teammate and close friend, Mark Meyer, was unable to compete. He had fought the previous year with a torn ACL, and needed to have it repaired. Madieyna Diouf got busy with work and school constraints, and he was also out. I immediately called my friend and training partner of fifteen years, Kyle Harder. Kyle, along with his brother Scott, was a young rambunctious eleven-year-old in Sensei Ray Hughes' Wado karate school when we first met, about fifteen years ago.

All heart, Meyer fought in 2007 with no ACL.

Both of these kids were somewhat boisterous, and obnoxious. Needless to say, I put them in them through their paces in sparring practice. Kyle had become an outstanding competitor, a grown man, and was winning many tournaments in Arizona. It is funny how the tide had changed. He was now administering the beatings and I was receiving them. He was no Diouf though, and did not have the timing of Meyer, but he was still pretty good.

I also called on Jeff "Freight Train" Dodge, who had quit karate after growing disenchanted in Shojiro Koyama's dojo. Freight Train was a really interesting addition because he's so fast and strong and talented, but it seems that no one ever told him what to do with those attributes. He used to be on a team opposing ours, and he and I had several knockdown, drag-out wars. I once punched him in the face as hard as I could and he got so mad at me, he tried to kick me right off the stage. When I asked him to join us, he became an enemy and a teammate at the same time, as I was not able to quickly let go of our rugged past.

The last order of business was to call on a favor from my old training partner Jason Berbaum. I had trained with Jason on and off for eighteen years, since the time he was a childhood karate prodigy. I begged Jason to come coach us. He has a gift for caring for and loving people, and he sees things karate-wise that many are not talented enough to see. I knew he could teach us and that the other guys who did not even know him would give him a fair chance to help us all get better. Jason is that special of a guy. Thankfully, he agreed.

All totaled, according to credentials, this team was inferior to the one that placed third the year before. I knew for us to win we would have to go above and beyond putting together a collection of superstars and hoping they would win. That's exactly what we did.

We all attended every tournament we could possibly compete in, no matter how small. We traveled to different states by van and to the far end of the country by plane. We E-mailed each other every day. We discussed what we wanted to get out of workouts and I planned those workouts in a logical systematic progression. We made DVDs of every tournament and our coach Jason watched them with the diligence of an NFL football coach. He came to the dojo with pages of written notes on each individual and drills each needed to improve. We made posters announcing team results to be hung in the dojo. We ran seminars to earn money for sweat suits and travel. I was astounded by how close this group of individuals had become: an African, a well-off white kid from Scottsdale, a brilliant Chinese guy, an old man, and a knuckle head we called the Freight Train. We started out as a team and grew to care so much about each other that we became a TEAM. For the 2008 Championships, one of our training partners, Yoko Ishida, made us hand-painted T-shirts with the Japanese characters for the word "family." This is precisely the way we functioned, as a family. Legendary basketball coach John Wooden said it best, that "true team spirit is a consideration for others, an eagerness to sacrifice personal interest or glory for the welfare of the team." We were becoming that team.

It is not as if we didn't have our trials. In most tournaments, we all easily won the preliminary rounds. This left us to fight each other violently in the final rounds. These fights often resulted in injuries, bleeding, and pain. In one tournament, Freight Train kicked Kyle so hard in the arm he broke it.

We often had to fight each other. In this case, Jihone was dining on Freight Train's right hand.

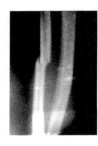

Kyle's fractured ulna, courtesy of his own teammate.

We also came very close to losing the first round of the 2008 National Championships. Down two matches to one, Jeff Dodge and I looked at each other with disbelief. We knew we were the fourth and fifth fighters, that our

Photo by Ryan Hunter

top three fighters had lost two out of three, and that one of us had to win and the other needed at least a tie to send our team into overtime. Otherwise, we would send ourselves back to Phoenix, losers for the 25th consecutive year. Our TEAM won both that match and the 2008 National Championships.

To my teammates. For thirty years I have played on teams and have watched coaches try to put together what we pulled off. You guys will always be my family and I will never forget the valuable lessons I learned from you. I love you all. Thank you to my TEAM, as well as those who trained with us (Sean Greene, T-Bone, Enesa, Yoko, Liz). We spent a year tired, sore, bleeding and beat up. It was worth every minute of it.

Brothers forever: the power of teamwork.
McClellan, Ekrissin, Dodge, Du, Harder, Coach Berbaum

Chapter 59

LESSONS FROM THE CONNECTOR
ANDREW CHAVEZ

"He is richest who is content with the least, for content is the wealth of nature."

   -Socrates

Photos by Nichole Chavez

My good friend, Jim Cope, referred Andrew Chavez to me. Jim is a sergeant with the Phoenix Police department and he works with Andrew's father, Jerry. Andrew himself was a high school senior who had just finished a great football season and won the state heavyweight championship in wrestling. Andrew had ambitions. He wanted to walk-on to Northern Arizona University's football team. He was also undersized to the point that he needed serious muscle growth and strength to accomplish this goal.

Andrew's father Jerry accompanied him on the first visit. I found Andrew bright, charming, articulate, and willing to work for his goal. He impressed me with his maturity, sincerity, professionalism, and class. We arranged a time for him to come lift, and I truly looked forward to training him.

At 4:00 in the afternoon the next day, a dirty, beat-up blazer flew into the parking lot and slammed on the breaks. Out jumped a Hispanic man covered from head to toe in cement dust, wearing a bandana over his head.

"Hey Coach, it's Andrew. Andrew Chavez," he said in a very Mexican

accent. "I'm ready to work for you." I couldn't believe this was Andrew. So professional twenty-four hours earlier, and now he looked like a mix between a beat-up construction worker and a gang member. Surprised, I told him to go change.

When Andrew returned, he told me he was ready to work and asked me to give him my best, something no athlete had ever asked me before. When curiosity got the better of me, I asked, "Andrew, it's not Halloween, what were you dressed up as?"

Andrew lifting high school wrestling coach, Dan Casey, after winning state championship.

"Oh, I was throwing cinder blocks all day for my grandfather," he said. "I think I moved over three hundred of them. Between that and my Mexican four-forty air conditioning I'm beat, but I really want your best."

Did this Hispanic young man really say, "Mexican four-forty air conditioning?" "Andrew, what is Mexican four-forty air conditioning?"

"Sorry coach, I forgot, with you being a white boy and all. Look at my truck. It's where you roll all four windows down and drive over 40 miles an hour," he said.

I wondered what I had on my hands. I worked him for three hours, and as per request, I gave him my best. I had him panting like a dog, sweating profusely, and dry heaving over a waste basket, but he came back for more.

A few sessions later, I was still giving him my best and he was still panting profusely and dry heaving. He started with the Mexican pitch again. Rarely do athletes initiate messing around with me and I've never had one make jokes about his own race. But Andrew Chavez was good natured and fun loving, hardworking, and he could get away from it. He would mock me for not understanding him and his "beautiful people," and tell me I was incomplete for not knowing Spanish. I did the only thing I could think of.

"Pipe down, Feo," I said. Yes, I used the word "feo," which means "ugly" in Spanish. Andrew was right, I did not know Spanish, but that stunned him a little. It happens that just a few months earlier I was told the story on how the kids in boxing coach Kenny Weldon's gym had a box-off, to see who could win the nickname Feo. The particular athlete who Kenny originally dubbed Feo had such a great work ethic, that he transformed himself from being a poor boxer, to the National Amateur Champion of the United States. This boxer's story has no correlation to my calling Andrew ugly, I was merely bluffing to shut him up as we had established a caring but playful relationship by then. In fact, I grew so fond of Andrew Chavez that I often found myself telling people I enjoyed training him as much as any of the other ten thousand athletes I had trained. He was that charismatic, that fun, and that hard working.

Andrew's life ended a few years later. The cause of death was meningitis. I attended his funeral, fighting the urge to cry hysterically over the death of the athlete I had grown to love. I saved the card handed out at the funeral, which says, "In Loving Memory. Andrew Chavez. February 25, 1988--June 19, 2008. 'Strength…great strength comes from faith in God.' Zechariah 12:5." I was awed by the number of people who came to his funeral, so many that every pew seat at the large church was filled, with hundreds standing in back. I realized then that Andrew didn't just have a special relationship with me, he had created those relationships with many, many people. I was touched. He had connected hundreds in his life, and again in his passing.

I kept the funeral card because I wanted a visual reminder of him. At the 2008 AAU National Karate Championship, I asked my wife Janet to sew the card between the patch and the karate gi top, essentially over my heart. With Andrew Chavez close to my heart, I would have the strength of a warrior and I would fight like one. He worked for me and I would work for him.

During those Championships, my nose broke and it bled profusely. A doctor asked if I wanted to stop the fight. A hard right hand also made me walk across the ring sideways as if drunk. No way would I stop fighting. With Andrew as a guardian angel, I continued until the fight ended. Having won, I got teary eyed thinking that Feo was watching and looking after me.

Four months after that contest, I took a few hours on a Saturday afternoon to write a letter to Andrew's father and his mother, Nichole. When I opened my mail box to mail the letter, I found an envelope with the name Chavez. I thought I was seeing things, but I wasn't. The letter came from Nichole, and reached me the exact day I wrote to her. The letter read:

Tim,

I would like you to know what an influence you had on Andrew's life. As our boys have grown, we have told them to always be themselves and proud of who they are without regard to the situation or environment they are in.

I remember the first day Andrew came home from his workout with you and said,

"Mom, Tim had me do some of the craziest things but they are really gonna help me, and, Mom, the best thing is he works with professional and college athletes and he treated me the same. He is like you always say, be who you are no matter the environment. I'm a kid from Laveen driving an old beat up Blazer and he still treated me the same as the ones with

Mercedes and Hummers."

When you gave him his nickname of "Feo," he was so proud that the two of you had a connection that not all of your clients had. The time Andrew spent with you was more than physical, it was character building and I thank you for that.

Typically parents speak at graduation and wedding parties to thank the people who had positive influences and molding their son to a man. God had Andrew as his chosen guardian and I did not want to miss the opportunity to say Thank You for your positive influence and role in Andrew's life!

With Deepest Gratitude,
    Nichole Chavez

I now know how Andrew had become the incredibly charismatic, outgoing, sincere, connector that he was. The apple doesn't fall far from the tree.

Andrew Chavez on top.

Chapter 60

▲

REVISITING
GARY HALL JR.

" Some things in life are worth looking at more than once. "
    -Unknown

Photo by Tim Clary/AFP/Getty Images

Some things in life stand out, and these are worth revisiting. For some, that may be a fine restaurant, a television show, or an entertainment act. For me, since high school, my favorite revisits were to Janet, who later became my wife. Every Friday night date was so enjoyable that I wanted to see her again on Saturday night.

The teacher I want to revisit now is one of the greatest guys I've ever had the fortune of meeting and learning from. This is Gary Hall Jr. I wrote about Gary back in Chapter 7 and wrote about the lesson of tolerance that I had learned from him. I referenced the public's perception of Gary, a perception created by the media, and how the perception is the polar opposite of the wonderful person I have had the pleasure to befriend and coach over the last seven years.

In my eyes, Gary's character is worth revisiting because there is so much of it. He never fails to impress me.

In 2007, I received an E-mail from a swimmer who specialized in the same events that Gary specialized in, the 50 meter freestyle and the 100 meter freestyle. The swimmer was none other than Roland Schoeman, the South African who had won gold, silver, and bronze in the 2004 Olympic Games. Roland had then gone on to break the world record in the 50 meter freestyle for short course, becoming the only person in history to swim 50 meters in less than 21 seconds. He wanted my help to prepare for the 2008 Beijing Olympic Games. I was flattered that he selected me at such an important time in his career. Gary had also asked me to prepare him for the 2008 Olympics.

Out of love and respect for Gary, I did the honorable thing and called Gary to see if he had a problem with me coaching a direct competitor.

"Gary, it's Tim. I need to ask a question of you. I've been contacted by a competitor of yours in both the 50 free and the 100 free, and he wants me to train him. If you don't want me to help him, or anybody else in the world in your events, let me know and I won't. I say this to you not because of your ability in the water but because of the friend you have been to me and the way you have treated me for the last seven years. Tell me what you want me to do."

Roland Schoeman, a shark in the water (Photo by Mike Aron).

"Who is it, Tim?" Gary asked.

"Roland Schoeman."

"Roland, huh." A brief moment of silence followed. "I like Roland," Gary said. "Make him fast."

I was astonished. Gary could easily have told me not to train Roland Schoeman. I think it safe to say most athletes would have chosen that option. He could have even said he could deal with it. Gary did neither of those. He told me to make his competitor fast. He responded in a way none of a thousand athletes questioned would have responded. But then again, that's Gary, a bit ahead of the rest of the world both in and out of the water.

FINAL THOUGHTS

"Actions speak louder than words."
  -Unknown

I have told real-life stories of people with extraordinary willpower, perseverance, and purpose. I have also shared stories about passion, love, and giving. The lessons I have learned have served to increase my inner strength, while strengthening my inner peace.

The fact is, there are many exceptional teachers in this world, ranging from young to old, athletically talented to non-athletic, and even from man to beast. We simply need to be cognizant of our teachers and the lessons they have to share.

Lessons learned are a gift. Lessons lived are even better. May all of your days be filled with blessings of both inner strength and inner peace.

ABOUT THE AUTHOR

 A self-described "ordinary guy with extraordinary determination," Tim McClellan, M.S., C.S.C.S.has distinguished himself worldwide during the past three decades as an innovator in the performance enhancement field. Among those he coached are more than 200 NFL players, 12 Olympic gold medalists, more than a dozen NCAA individual champions, 9 NCAA team champions, more than 200 NCAA All-Americans and National Champions of 17 different sports. Tim also coached at Arizona State University for 13 years and has worked with the USA Olympic wrestling team, the World Champion USA powerlifting team, and the Boston Bruins. He was honored by the National Strength and Conditioning Association in 1990 as a recipient of their President's Award.

A multiple National Champion himself in karate-do, Tim holds black belt ranks in five different martial arts. He has written numerous magazine articles and produced a variety of instructional videos.

ALSO FROM TIM MCCLELLAN

TRAINING PROGRAMS: Learn more about training programs similar to the ones the pros use at StrengthAndPeace.com

INSTRUCTIONAL VIDEO TAPES: Visit StrengthAndPeace.com

StrengthAndPeace.com

CPSIA information can be obtained
at www.ICGtesting.com
Printed in the USA
BVOW11s2351060816

458168BV00005B/67/P